User-Generated Content and its Impact on Branding

Severin Dennhardt

User-Generated Content and its Impact on Branding

How Users and Communities Create and Manage Brands in Social Media

Severin Dennhardt
Innsbruck, Austria

Dissertation University of Innsbruck, 2012

ISBN 978-3-658-02349-2   ISBN 978-3-658-02350-8 (eBook)
DOI 10.1007/978-3-658-02350-8

The Deutsche Nationalbibliothek lists this publication in the Deutsche Nationalbibliografie; detailed bibliographic data are available in the Internet at http://dnb.d-nb.de.

Library of Congress Control Number: 2013949475

Springer Gabler
© Springer Fachmedien Wiesbaden 2014
This work is subject to copyright. All rights are reserved by the Publisher, whether the whole or part of the material is concerned, specifically the rights of translation, reprinting, reuse of illustrations, recitation, broadcasting, reproduction on microfilms or in any other physical way, and transmission or information storage and retrieval, electronic adaptation, computer software, or by similar or dissimilar methodology now known or hereafter developed. Exempted from this legal reservation are brief excerpts in connection with reviews or scholarly analysis or material supplied specifically for the purpose of being entered and executed on a computer system, for exclusive use by the purchaser of the work. Duplication of this publication or parts thereof is permitted only under the provisions of the Copyright Law of the Publisher's location, in its current version, and permission for use must always be obtained from Springer. Permissions for use may be obtained through RightsLink at the Copyright Clearance Center. Violations are liable to prosecution under the respective Copyright Law.
The use of general descriptive names, registered names, trademarks, service marks, etc. in this publication does not imply, even in the absence of a specific statement, that such names are exempt from the relevant protective laws and regulations and therefore free for general use.
While the advice and information in this book are believed to be true and accurate at the date of publication, neither the authors nor the editors nor the publisher can accept any legal responsibility for any errors or omissions that may be made. The publisher makes no warranty, express or implied, with respect to the material contained herein.

Printed on acid-free paper

Springer Gabler is a brand of Springer DE.
Springer DE is part of Springer Science+Business Media.
www.springer-gabler.de

To my mother

Acknowledgements

*Research is to see what everybody else has seen,
and to think what nobody else has thought.*
Albert Szent-Gyorgyi

This thesis wouldn't have come to existence without the help and support of a lot of people. I would like to thank those here who contributed to the realization of this work.

I would like to thank my supervisor Univ.-Prof. Dr. Kurt Matzler for the opportunity to realize this dissertation project within the Department of Strategic Management and for his continuous support and valuable suggestions during the course of this work.

Special thanks go to Dr. Johann Füller and Dr. Thomas Kohler. They have introduced me to the world of research and provided me with outstanding guidance through the various stages of this dissertation. They always had time for my numerous questions and gave constructive feedback to all the drafts I send them. They also provided technical and operational assistance for the execution of my research projects. Hereby, I would also like to express my thanks to the Hyve AG in Munich for the invaluable support with the execution of one study.

I am also grateful for the support and help of the whole team at the Department of Strategic Management. I could always approach them with whatever questions I had and talking to them gave me a lot of valuable insights into research topics. During the last one and a half years they provided a true "research home" for me.

I am also deeply indebted to my family. Without their support, I wouldn't have been able to pursue the goal of a dissertation. They have always inspired and encouraged me to go my way. A special thank goes to my mother who always supported me with whatever plans I had. Special thanks also go to Albina, coping with me through the ups and downs of such a dissertation project.

Last, I would like to thank my employer McKinsey. If it wasn't for the *Fellow Programme*, I probably would have never considered tackling this project and would have missed many valuable experiences associated with it.

Severin Dennhardt

Outline

This thesis is entitled

User-generated Content and its Impact on Branding
How Users and Communities Create and Manage Brands

and is written as a doctoral dissertation in Social and Economic Sciences at the University of Innsbruck – School of Management. This cumulative dissertation consists of a number of published and unpublished articles and follows the standards for cumulative dissertations at the University of Innsbruck – School of Management.

This dissertation is divided into two sections. The first section, Part A, outlines the objectives of this research, provides a general theoretical background for the topic and gives an overview of the methodology concerning the studies conducted. The second section, Part B, presents each of the four individual papers comprised in this dissertation. Further, this part delivers a summary of the major research contributions and implications of the work included in this thesis.

Table of Contents

Acknowledgements .... **VII**

Outline .... **IX**

Part A – Research Overview 1

1 Introduction 3
   1.1 Problem Identification 3
   1.2 Research Objectives 7
   1.3 Structure of the Thesis 9

2 Theoretical Framework 11
   2.1 Co-creation of Brands 11
   2.2 The Value of Brands 12
   2.3 Social Capital Theory 14
   2.4 Purchase Decision-making Process and the Hierarchy of Effects 16

3 Research Setting 19

4 Methodology 23
   4.1 Content Analysis Based on Qualitative Interviews 24
   4.2 Experiment 25
   4.3 Structural Equation Modeling Based on Online Survey Data 25

Part B – Articles Contributing to this Doctoral Thesis 27

5 Overview of Papers Included in Doctoral Thesis 29
   5.1 Paper 1: User-generated Brands Emerging from Social Media: What Corporate Brands can Learn from Brand Management in Virtual Worlds 29
   5.2 Paper 2: Perception of User-generated Brands: A New Power in the Minds of Consumers? 30

- 5.3 Paper 3: The Value-enhancing Role of Social Networks Around Brands: The Concept of Social Brand Value 30
- 5.4 Paper 4: The Impact of Social Media on Brand Awareness .... 31 and Purchase Intention: The Case of MINI on Facebook 31

6 User-generated Brands: What Corporate Brands Can Learn from Brand Management in Virtual Worlds 33
- 6.1 Introduction 33
- 6.2 Theoretical Foundations 34
  - 6.2.1 Definition and Core Characteristics of Brands 34
  - 6.2.2 User-generated Brands 36
  - 6.2.3 Affordances of Virtual Worlds for User-generated Brands 37
- 6.3 Empirical Study 40
  - 6.3.1 Research Method 40
  - 6.3.2 Results 42
- 6.4 Discussion 47
- 6.5 Conclusions 50
- 6.6 Appendix – Interviewguideline 54

7 Perception of User-generated Brands: A New Power in the Minds of Consumers? 57
- 7.1 Introduction 57
- 7.2 Conceptual Foundations 58
  - 7.2.1 The Value of Brands for Consumers 58
  - 7.2.2 Utility of User Generated Brands 59
- 7.3 Method and Study Design 61
- 7.4 Results 62
- 7.5 Discussion, Implications and Limitations 64

8 The Value-enhancing Role of Social Networks Around Brands: The Concept of Social Brand Value 67
- 8.1 Introduction 67
- 8.2 Theoretical Background 69
  - 8.2.1 The Brand Equity Concept 69
  - 8.2.2 Social Capital and the Creation of Value through Relationships and Interactions 71
  - 8.2.3 Social Capital of Brands 72

	8.3	Conceptual Model	74
		8.3.1 Quality and its Impact on Brand Value	74
		8.3.2 Social Brand Value	75
	8.4	Empirical Study	78
		8.4.1 Research Setting	78
		8.4.2 Measures	79
		8.4.3 Descriptive Analysis	80
		8.4.4 Results	83
	8.5	Discussion	87
	8.6	Limitations and Future Research	90
9	**The Impact of User Interactions in Social Media on Brand Awareness and Purchase Intention: The Case of MINI on Facebook**		**91**
	9.1	Introduction	91
	9.2	Consumers as Co-creators of Brands	92
	9.3	Purchase Decision-making Process	93
	9.4	Conceptual Model and Hypothesis Development	96
	9.5	Empirical Study and Analysis	100
		9.5.1 Data Collection	100
		9.5.2 Measures	100
		9.5.3 Results	101
	9.6	Discussion and Implications	103
	9.7	Limitations and Outlook	105
10	**Contributions and Implications**		**107**
	10.1 Theoretical Implications		107
	10.2 Managerial Implications		110
11	**Limitations and Future Research**		**113**
12	**References**		**115**
	Article Overview		**129**

Part A – Research Overview

1 Introduction

The emergence and rise of social media have made user-generated content one of the driving forces of online experiences today. User-generated content (UGC, also called user-created content or user-generated media), for example in the form of user-reviews or blog-posts, is one of the most influential sources of online information today (Constantinides and Fountain 2008). The widespread penetration of web 2.0 applications, in combination with faster and greater mobile computing power and advances in bandwidth, has been the driver behind the revolution of user-generated content and applications based on it. This change in the (marketing) communication environment presents both opportunities and challenges for firms and their brand management (Hoffman and Fodor 2010). Marketers have to deal with the growing uncontrollable influence of consumers (Bernoff and Li 2008), which they exert through user-generated content or even user-generated brands.

1.1 Problem Identification

Fueled by web 2.0 technologies and the pervasion of UGC, brands created by users and user communities have become a contemporary phenomenon. Users thereby contribute their leisure time and creative energy to the development of products, which ultimately leads to the generation of brands. Examples of this phenomenon include well known software and online brands. Apache and Linux present the best known examples of user-generated brands. In their case, communities of software developers invested their leisure time to contribute to the development of software programs. Another UGB example is Wikipedia. Here, users have invested their spare time to collect and make available information and knowledge in form of an online dictionary. In the virtual world Second Life (SL), various users have also established their own brands. Gothicatz or Stiletto Moody are two brands in the SL fashion industry that were created by users out of love for fashion and being creative and a need for tailored products. The founders thereby started by developing products for their own use and ended up by selling the products to other users. The core driver behind all these brands – their creation and management – is UGC.

UGC – defined as online content that is publicly available and created by end-users in a creative effort – and its manifestation in social media applications has recently attracted much research interest (Constantinides and Fountain 2008; Keller 2009). Investigated topics include the impact of user-reviews on consumer behavior (cp. Chen et al. 2011; Mudambi and Schuff 2010; Zhu and Zhang 2010), social media as a driving force of consumer empowerment (cp. Cova et al. 2011; Merz et al. 2009), users as innovators and producers (cp. Franke and Shah 2003; von Hippel 2005), and the building and influence of brand communities (cp. Muniz and O'Guinn 2001; Schau et al. 2009). However, the impact and relevance of UGC and social media for brands and their management has yet to be better understood.

Firms are facing a new communication reality that has been created by the rise of social media. Social media is thereby defined as "a group of Internet-based applications that build on the ideological foundations of web 2.0, and that allow the creation and exchange of User Generated Content" (Kaplan and Haenlein 2010, p. 63). The term covers many Internet-based applications such as blogs, social networking sites, content communities, virtual game worlds and virtual social worlds (cp. Kim et al. 2009; Smith 2009).

Yet, there is little knowledge and consensus on how brands can or should be developed in the modern interactive marketplace (Constantinides and Fountain 2008; Hoffman and Fodor 2010; Keller 2009). For the management of brands, these new developments in the way people communicate with each other present both opportunities and challenges (Bernoff and Li 2008; Keller and Richey 2006). With consumers spending more time on platforms such as Facebook, Youtube or Twitter, an increasing share of the interaction with and the experience around brands occurs within these new communication environments (Henderson and Bowley 2010). Because content in these social media environments is created and co-created by users interactively, individuals and communities increasingly have the power to influence existing brands (Holt 2002; Kane et al. 2009; Muniz and Schau 2007; OECD 2007; Thompson et al. 2006). This is adding a new dimension to branding and marketing communications, challenging the way brands communicate and interact with their customers (Barwise and Meehan 2010; Bernoff and Li 2008; Constantinides and Fountain 2008; Cova et al. 2011; Engagementdb 2009; Keller 2009).

While large brands are still struggling to get a grip on their social media efforts, individual users have demonstrated that creating brands within user-generated online environments is possible. Brands that originated from single users or a group of users through user-generated content, rather than companies,

1.1 Problem Identification

are called user-generated brands (UGB). They are defined as brands that are created – originally unintentionally – by communities of users or single users outside of their professional routines in social media environments, where their products are publicly available and show a creative effort. Recently, this notion that users can establish businesses and brands is gaining traction (Pitt et al. 2006; Schroll et al. 2010; von Hippel et al. 2011). This trend is supported by findings on innovation activities by users (von Hippel 2005) and research that has identified innovative users to become "accidental" entrepreneurs (Shah and Tripsas 2007). In brand research the notion of the influential and active user has also been recognized. Brands today are described as the product of a complex social process involving various stakeholders (Merz et al. 2009; Vargo and Lusch 2004). The power and momentum salient in the co-creation process has also been described with respect to brand communities, where users of a brand share a collective passion for this brand, interact with each other around it, and thereby eventually create value for the brand (Schau et al. 2009).

To the present date, literature on brands that are created by users, rather than simply influenced, modified or captured by them, is rare. Pitt et al. (2006) point out that the Open Source movement has produced some well known brands like Apache and Linux, which were effectively created and established by users and which exhibit features "like any other" brand (p. 115). Füller et al. (2008) found that online communities of users sharing a specific interest were developing customized products within their community and were thereby building meaningful and enchanting brands for the community. Research on the Apache brand further developed that concept by showing that community brands also create strong associations outside of the user-community (Schroll et al. 2010; von Hippel et al. 2011). Investigating the emergence and characteristics of UGBs in virtual worlds (VW) could add to this research in providing valuable insights on effects and implications on branding in social media environments.

Within virtual worlds, successful brands have been created by users – often outperforming established corporations (de Mesa 2009). Since VWs like Second Life enable users to exchange services as well as virtual goods (Mennecke et al. 2009) and thereby give users the opportunity to create and capture the value of their efforts, VWs provide ideal premises for the creation of UGBs. VWs therefore present an exemplary field to study the phenomenon of UGBs, as they provide an economic "playing" ground where users can freely and easily set up own businesses and build brands.

The example of VWs shows that user-generated brands exhibit value to consumers. Although UGBs outside of virtual worlds have been recognized and accepted by consumers (e.g., Apache, Linux, etc.), commercialization has mostly not occurred. Since the value of UGBs is therefore hard to capture in financial terms, it has to be evaluated in terms of utility for consumers. The value of brands for consumers can be derived from the benefits or functions a brand possesses: the risk reduction function (Keller 2008), the symbolic function (Escalas and Bettman 2003; Levy 1959), and the social function. Whereas the first benefit is primarily a functional one, the second one illustrates that brands can also serve as social symbols (Fischer et al. 2010) and cultural resources (Holt 2002). These characteristics confer brands the ability to express the self and to help consumers create and build their self-identities (Escalas and Bettman 2005). Social benefits of brands originate in its ability to connect people and, hence, to be a resource for social capital (Bourdieu 1986; Bourdieu 1989; Muniz and O'Guinn 2001). Value is thereby created through and lies within the interactions of all stakeholders and the collectively perceived value-in-use of brands (Cova et al. 2007; Merz et al. 2009). Research so far has not looked at the value creating utility of brands created by users and has thereby not investigated if and what kind of a potential competitive advantage those brands exhibit.

One of the proposed value components of UGBs is derived from the social utility they provide to consumers. Previous research has argued that brands exhibit a value enhancing social nature, which indirectly contributes to brand equity (Muniz and O'Guinn 2001). However, to this point, it remains unclear how important the ability of brands to foster social interactions is to consumers, how it might influence the valuation of brands, and how this value could be measured. So far, research on concepts for measuring brand value from a consumer's perspective – mainly the brand equity concept (Keller 1993) – has not included a social, relationship-based perspective on the value of brands for consumers. Bourdieu's (1986) theory of social capital presents a theoretical foundation to investigate the social role brands play in consumers' lives and to develop a concept that captures this value.

Since consumers are increasingly active in social media and user-generated content has a strong influence on opinion-forming social media content increasingly influences purchase decisions. Prior studies have shown that social media presents a potentially powerful and cost effective tool for marketing communication (Engagementdb 2009; Hinz et al. forthcoming; Kozinets et al. 2010). People rely more than ever on their social networks when making purchase decisions (Hinz et al. forthcoming). Since an increasing part of this network is situated within the social media space and a large part of the communication within the network is happening in this space, SM platforms exhibit an important role in consumer decision-making (Constantinides and Fountain 2008). Facebook and Co. therefore present a new key playing field for brands. However, outcomes of social media activities are still disputed in practice (Hoffman and Fodor 2010). The effects of social media campaigns on consumers' perception of products and brands as well as the effects on the purchase decision-making process have yet to be better understood and described by research (Barwise and Meehan 2010; Edelman 2010). In theory and practice the question remains if the outcomes justify the investments.

1.2 Research Objectives

The goal of this thesis is to close the gaps identified in current research and to overcome some of the fundamental issues that prevent us from fully understanding the role of social media and user-generated content in creating and managing brands.

First, this study seeks to identify popular brands that emerged from users' initiatives and aims at identifying their characteristics. Taking the example of virtual worlds, users have shown that creating successful brands is doable and frequently their initiatives have outperformed established corporations (de Mesa 2009). The goal of this thesis is to show the existence of these grassroots brands, identify their common characteristics, and answer the question of why these brands emerge and what their competitive advantage is. Thereby our understanding of brands and brand management within virtual worlds and social media will be enhanced. This work thereby also attempts to generate insights for brand management practitioners dealing with virtual worlds and social media.

Second, this research aims to test what kind of utility user-generated brands have for consumers, how consumers value this utility, and how it differentiates UGBs from corporate brands. This study therefore investigates the psychological, sociological, and practical benefits of those brands for consumers as potential drivers of competitive advantage. It has been suggested that brands created by users exhibit value beyond what large commercial brands can offer. However, no study has empirically tested what kind of utility those brands possess and how they are perceived in comparison to corporate brands. It is the goal of this thesis to show that the origin of a brand as user-generated has an influence on how consumers perceive a brand with respect to sympathy, authenticity, and credibility.

Third, building on research that argued for a social nature of brands (Muniz and O'Guinn 2001) and social capital theory (Bourdieu 1986), this study introduces the Social Brand Value (SBV) construct to measure the social value of brands and demonstrates that social aspects have an influence on consumers' valuation of the brand. To this point, it is unclear how consumers value the ability of brands to foster social interactions and how this might influence the valuation of brands. Given the importance of social ties, social interactions, and social identity in the new media environment, there is a growing need to account for a relationship measure in contemporary marketing and branding. This study therefore investigates how the social attractiveness of a brand for consumers influences their valuation of the brand and if practice should account for a social measure when evaluating brands.

Finally, this thesis investigates the effects of social media marketing activities for important brand constructs. Outcomes of social media activities are still disputed in practice (Hoffman and Fodor 2010). In brand management the question about social media's importance and relevance for marketing remains unresolved (Barwise and Meehan 2010; Edelman 2010). Simultaneously, UGBs have shown that by relying mainly on social media marketing, meaningful brands can be created. Through the investigation of a car manufacturer's Facebook activities, this thesis aims to demonstrate that social media marketing has positive effects on consumers' brand attitude and purchase intention. It thereby shows that social media and UGC have similar effects compared to other marketing communication tools as they influence brand awareness, positive word-of-mouth, and consumers' purchase intentions. It thereby also demonstrates the effectiveness of UGBs marketing activities.

Consequently, this thesis aims to contribute to the branding literature by addressing the following research questions:

1) What are defining characteristics of user-generated brands in social media environments and what can be inferred from those characteristics for brand management?

2) Does the user-generated nature of a brand influence its perception of consumers with regard to authenticity, credibility, and sympathy?

3) How can the social value of a brand be measured and how do consumers value the social nature of brands?

4) How are consumers' brand related awareness, purchase intention, and word-of-mouth activity affected by fanpage involvement and brand page annoyance?

1.3 Structure of the Thesis

This thesis is structured in two main parts. After introducing the objectives of this research, Part A continues by outlining the objectives of this research, providing a general theoretical background for the topic and giving an overview of the methodology employed for conducting the studies.

Chapter 2 will give an overview of the theoretical concepts that were applied in this study. Focus will be given to utilities and value of brands; to the social value of brands as an important component of brand value and social capital theory as a source of explanation; and to theories behind consumers' purchase decision process. Chapter 2 will thereby highlight where gaps in our understanding of branding processes in light of contemporary technological and social developments are.

Following the description of the theoretical background, chapter 3 will then give a short overview on the particular research settings. Chapter 4 will outline the research designs applied during the course of the thesis. Also, a description of the methodologies used to answer the identified research questions will be given in this chapter.

Part B of this dissertation presents each of the four individual research projects included in this dissertation. In chapter 4 the six published and unpublished articles and an overview of their most important findings will be given (see Table 1). The original copies of the four relevant articles will be presented in full length in the appendix. Chapter 5 provides an integration of the findings of these individual papers and provides a comprehensive discussion of the major contributions and managerial implications. Finally, chapter 6 concludes with a summary of limitations immanent to the findings in combination with an outlook for future research opportunities.

Table 1: Article overview and attributed points

Nr.	Publication	Journal/Conference-Proceedings	Authors	Points	Formula to be applied	Status	Points if accepted
1.1	User-generated Brands: What Brand Management can Learn from Virtual Worlds	40th European Marketing Academy Conference (EMAC), Ljubljana, May 24-27, 2011	Dennhardt, S.; Kohler, Th.; Füller, J.	0,6*	3/(3+2)*1	accepted	0,6*
1.2	User-generated Brands Emerging from Social Media: What Corporate Brands can Learn from Brand Management in Virtual Worlds (substantially extended and revised version of 1.1)	Information Systems Journal *Impact Factor: 3.020*	Dennhardt, S.; Kohler, Th.; Füller, J.	0,6	3/(3+2)*1	submitted	3/(3+2)*3=1,8
2	Perception of User-generated Brands: A New Power in the Minds of Consumers?	19th International Product Development Management Conference (IPDMC), Manchester, June 17-19, 2012	Dennhardt, S.	1	1	accepted	1
3.1	Social Brand Value and the Value Enhancing Role of Social Media Relationships for Brands	45th Hawaii International Conference on System Sciences (HICSS), Hawaii, January 4-7, 2012	Füller, J.; Schroll, R.; Dennhardt, S.; Hutter, K.	0,5*	3/(4+2)*1	accepted	0,5*
3.2	The Value-Enhancing Role of Social Networks Around Brands: The Concept of Social Brand Value (substantially extended and revised version of 3.1)	Journal of Marketing *Impact Factor: 7.243*	Füller, J.; Dennhardt, S.; Schroll, R.; Hutter, K.	0,5	3/(4+2)*1	submitted	3/(4+2)*3=1,5
4	The impact of Social Media on Brand Awareness and Purchase Intention: The Case of MINI on Facebook	41th European Marketing Academy Conference (EMAC), Lisbon, May 22-25, 2012	Füller, J.; Hautz, J.; Dennhardt, S.; Hutter, K.	0,5	3/(4+2)*1	submitted	0,5
	Total			2,6			4,8

2 Theoretical Framework

To the present date, no comprehensive theory for user-generated content and its impact on branding exists. In this section, theories and approaches will be described that were used to answer the research questions on the emergence of user-generated brands and the influence of social media on branding.

2.1 Co-creation of Brands

Marketing literature in the last decade has undergone a shift towards a service-dominant logic (Vargo and Lusch 2004). This logic puts the customer back into the center of marketing theory as it implies that the value of an offering (product or service) is defined and co-created with the consumer instead of being embedded in the output per se (Vargo and Lusch 2008). Consumers are not perceived as passive participants anymore but as active shapers and contributors in marketing. The notion of the prosumer (Kotler 1986) has become a synonym for the value-creation relationship between firms and customers.

This new perspective in marketing is also reflected in the contemporary understanding of brands. The creation of brands is now viewed as an ongoing social process (Füller et al. 2012; Muniz and O'Guinn 2001), whereby value is co-created in the interplay and negotiations of various stakeholders (Merz et al. 2009). This process encompasses a system consisting of brand meaning, manifestations of this meaning, and the various stakeholders as the relevant actors (Mühlbacher et al. 2006). As shown by the brand community literature (Brown et al. 2003; Muniz and O'Guinn 2001; Schau et al. 2009), brand value is created through collective experiences and interpretations enabled by relationships based on brands. Brand value is therefore "also co-created through network relationships and social interactions among the ecosystem of all the stakeholders" (Merz et al. 2009, p. 338). Brand literature has evolved from a brand logic that viewed brands as simple markers of identification and value as inherent in goods determined by the value-in-exchange, to a new logic that views brands as being complex social phenomena (Brown et al. 2003; Holt 2002; Kozinets 2002; Pitt et al. 2006) and the value of brands as its collectively perceived value-in-use (Franke and Piller 2004; Schau et al. 2009).

The social nature of brands (Muniz and O'Guinn 2001) and the relevance of relationships in co-creating brand value (Kozinets et al. 2008; McAlexander et al. 2002) enhance the importance of social media as a marketing channel. Social media favors relationship and community building as well as it promotes active engagements of consumers. The direct involvement social media enables in respect to the creation of brand value gives consumers ever more power to influence brands and posits challenges for brand managers' efforts to manage their brand. Furthermore, the ease of online brand-community building and the value those communities provide for consumers as well as firms, has become another important aspect of brand management. Therefore marketing activities within social media environments have to take into account and work with the increased power of consumers.

2.2 The Value of Brands

Brands are among the most valuable assets companies possess and hence the management of their value is of top priority for firms. Value for the owner of brands lies within a brand's ability to generate financial profits and to establish a competitive advantage by differentiating itself from competitors (Keller 2008; Riesenbeck and Perrey 2007). For consumers the value of brands is based on the functions and utilities they represent (de Chernatony and Riley 1998; Kapferer 2008). In other words, a brand's perceived value for a consumer is the total sum of the physical and psychological benefits the consumer receives from the brand (Avery et al. 2010). This perceived value stems from four distinct benefit dimensions: informational benefits, risk reducing benefits, symbolic and identity related benefits, and social benefits.

First, brands are carriers of information (cp. Kapferer 2008; Keller 2008). They let consumers easily recognize and identify products and give them information about the origin and quality of the product. They thereby lower search costs as they allow time and energy-saving through repurchasing and loyalty.

Secondly, brands lower consumers' perceived risk of making a wrong purchase decision. They indicate a certain level of quality, ensure the expected performance, and attest social acceptance (cp. Kapferer 2008; Riesenbeck and Perrey 2007). Physical and psychological risks perceived by the consumer that are imminent in every purchase decision are thereby reduced. To serve these two rather mechanical functions, brands need to be perceived by consumers as trustworthy and as having the necessary expertise.

Third, brands support consumers in their creation of self-concept and social identity and therefore exhibit a symbolic function (Ahuvia 2005; Belk 1988; Escalas and Bettman 2005; Fournier 1998). For consumers, brands are a powerful source of meaning (Fournier 1998) and, hence, serve as powerful symbolic and cultural resources for individual identity projects (Holt 2002; McCracken 1989). For instance, brands can enhance individual identities through associations with certain social realities and standards (Grubb and Hupp 1968). Consumers tend to prefer brands with characteristics that match their own as they are better suited for identity building (Aaker et al. 2004). Put differently, consumers' brand preference interrelates with the connection of the own self with the brand (Escalas and Bettman 2005). The greater the congruity or connection between consumers' own personal characteristics and those of the brand is, the greater is the preference for the brand (Aaker 1997). Self-brand connection has been found to influence important variables such as brand attitude, brand choice, and store loyalty (Helgeson and Supphellen 2004; Sirgy et al. 1997). To serve as valuable ingredients of meaning for the creation of identity, brands must be perceived as authentic and sympathetic by consumers and must be offered as cultural resources (Holt 2002).

Fourth, and yet not widely acknowledged, brands exhibit a social function as they support the building of relationships and social ties and foster social integration (Cova 1997; Muniz and O'Guinn 2001; Schau et al. 2009). Research into brand communities demonstrates that a shared consciousness, rituals and traditions, and a sense of moral responsibility form and hold together affectionate communities around brands (Muniz and Schau 2005). Cova (1997) argues that consumers value products and services less for their use-value and more for their linking-value – for their ability to enable and facilitate bonds between individuals. A recent study by Füller et al. (2012) shows that brands exhibit a social value as they help consumers build social capital.

The relevance and utility of brands in consumer society change over time against the background of societal developments. Fournier (1996) for example described the role of brands in postmodern society as follows: "Relationships with mass brands can soothe the 'empty selves' left behind by society's abandonment of tradition and community and provide stable anchors in an otherwise changing world. The formation and maintenance of brand-product relationships serve many culturally-supported roles within postmodern society" (p. 1).Hence, current societal post-postmodernistic developments are also likely to influence the role and utility of brands.

2.3 Social Capital Theory

Bourdieu (1984) described the social world as a multidimensional space in which differentiation happens through various types of resources or capital from which people draw. It follows that this social space is structured according to the distribution of various forms of capital, which have the capability to confer strength and power and consequently profit their holder. Bourdieu (1986) essentially differentiates among three types of capital: economic, cultural, and social capital. Economic capital comprises everything that is "immediately and directly convertible into money" (Bourdieu 1986, p. 243) and is institutionalized in the form of property rights. Cultural capital consists of "socially rare and distinctive tastes, skills, knowledge, and practices" (Holt 1998, p. 3) and appears in three primary forms embodied as "implicit practical knowledge, skills, and disposetions; objectified in cultural objects; and institutionalized in official degrees and diplomas" (Holt 1998, p. 3). Social capital is defined as the entirety of actual and potential resources that arise from more or less durable networks of institutionalized relationships (Bourdieu 1986). In other words, social capital gives its holder access to resources embedded in social networks that he may use and from which he may profit (Esser 2008; Lin 2001). Economic capital can be used to build the latter two forms of capital through efforts of transformation. Conversely, cultural and social capital exhibit value for the holder as they convey status and can be converted, under certain conditions, into economic capital (Bourdieu 1986). In respect to social capital, an individual holder can use his social relations to borrow or capture other actors' resources in order to generate profit for himself (Lin 2001). For example, a social actor might get valuable information concerning a lucrative investment opportunity, or he might be able to get better medical treatment through his relations to top-class doctors. The ability to convert social capital thereby depends on the structural position of the actor in the network, the strength of the ties within the network, the purpose of access (i.e., instrumental or for maintaining cohesion, solidarity, or well-being) and the skills in conducting the conversion (Lin 2001).

In contrast to the other forms of capital, social capital is purely relational, as it entails resources based on membership to social groups (Vogt 2000). The profits, which accrue through this membership, are the basis for solidarity, which in turn makes the profits possible (Bourdieu 1986). These profits or returns arise from three typical forms of social resources and benefits provided by relations and networks: social integration, symbolic or identity value, and access to knowledge. First, through membership to a group or community, individuals in the network experience mutual trust, solidarity and support (Esser 2008), and receive social credentials (Lin 2001). Second, as relations based on interactions form social capital, and as identity is a product of interactions and highly dependable on the social space in which these interactions take place, social capital plays a central role in the building of people's identity and therefore exhibits identity value to the holder (Lin 2001; Vogt 2000). Third, social capital presents value to its holder as it grants access to knowledge and information within social networks (Esser 2008; Lin 2001).

Relationships and ties formed in an online environment create (social) value as they represent social capital. Value-creating relationships that constitute social capital are thereby independent of the proximity of these relations in geographical, economic, or social space (Bourdieu 1986). Therefore, it doesn't matter if the relevant network ties are situated in an offline or online context. As relationships today are significantly influenced by developments of de-traditionalization and individualization (Vogt 2000), and as social interactions are happening increasingly in online environments, social online networks play an increasingly important role in the creation of people's social capital.

The connection between social capital theory and branding theory is grounded within the social nature of brands and its encompassing benefits for customers. Because of the social function of brands, consumption and preference of a brand can help in building relationships and forming a sense of community (McAlexander et al. 2002, Muniz and O'Guinn 2001). Social connections, enabled by brand communities and other brand-related relationships, represent potentially valuable resources for consumers and therefore increase the value of the brand for consumers and, hence, for companies. By applying Bourdieu's theory of capital, the value consumers receive from social interactions and relations in connection with a brand can be described as part of consumers' social capital. Brands present to consumers a way to interact and relate to other consumers and thus to build social capital. Hence, one of the main purposes a brand today is consumed is for its ability to serve as a means for social integration, identity building, and information access. Through these profit sources, consumers receive additional returns for the social capital a brand represents. Putting it differently, the social capital a brand offers stems from being relevant in social networks and, thereby, providing individuals the possibilities to connect and interact with each other about the meaning and experiences that a brand offers.

2.4 Purchase Decision-making Process and the Hierarchy of Effects

The consumer decision-making process comprises various steps a consumer passes through when making a purchase decision. This process encompasses all steps from the recognition of a need through the pre-purchase search for information about potential ways to satisfy the need, the evaluation of alternative options to the actual purchase and the post-purchase processes including experience and evaluation of the product (Olshavsky and Granbois 1979; Schiffman and Kanuk 1991).

Similar to the framework of the decision-making process are the "hierarchy of effects" (HOE) models in communication and advertising. Instead of describing the series of steps a consumer runs through when making a purchase decision, those models focus on the mental stages of the relationship of consumers with a specific product or brand (Mooradian et al. 2012; Ray 1973). Hierarchy of effects refers to the fixed order in which consumers perceive, process and use advertising and other marketing communication information: first, cognitively (thinking); second, affectively (feeling); and third, conatively (doing) (Barry and Howard 1990). This means that the consumer first attains awareness and knowledge about a product, subsequently develops positive or negative feelings towards the product and finally acts by buying and using or by rejecting and avoiding the product(Kotler and Keller 2010). This kind of persuasive model argues for a hierarchical order in which things happen, with the implication that the earlier effects have a stronger impact on consumer's decision-making (Vakratsas and Ambler 1999). Based on this idea a variety of models has been proposed, differing in most cases only in nomenclature or order of effects (Barry and Howard 1990; Vakratsas and Ambler 1999).

The best-known hierarchy of effects model is AIDA, which consists of the purchase decision or attitude building phases **a**wareness, **i**nterest, **d**esire, and **a**ction. Another widely recognized model is the one by Lavidge and Steiner (1961) (Figure 1). They included into their model the phases awareness, knowledge, liking, preference, conviction, and purchase. At the beginning of the modeled process, the consumer is unaware of the brand. In the next phase he becomes aware of the existence of the brand, but has not yet formed any knowledge. Next, the consumer receives (e.g., through advertising or word-of-mouth) or searches for information about the brand on which basis he learns what the brand has to offer and builds knowledge. After going through the "thinking"

2.4 Purchase Decision-making Process and the Hierarchy of Effects

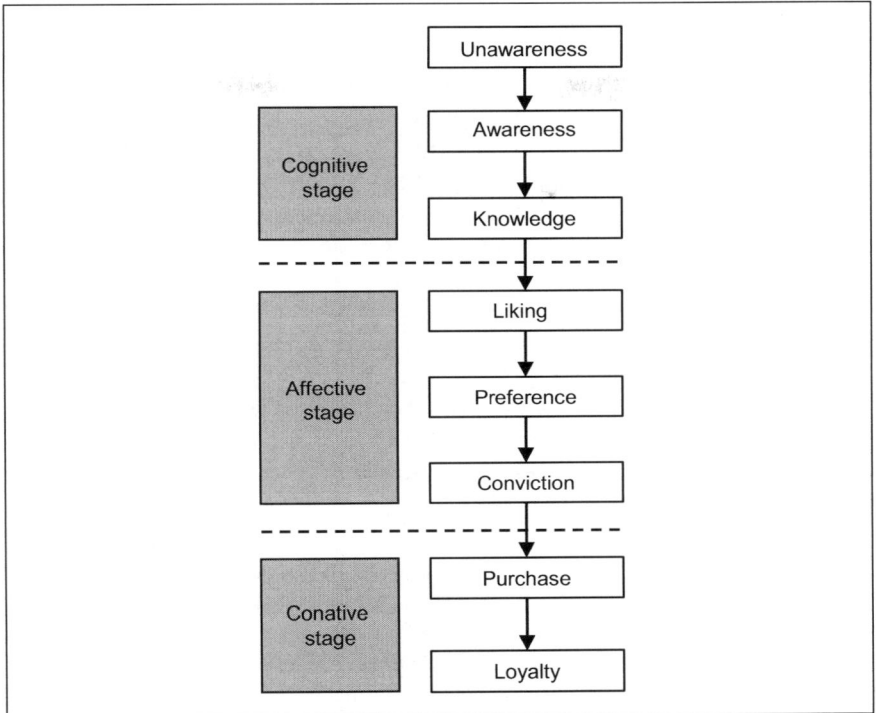

Figure 1: Hierarchy of effects model

stage, the consumer decides in the affective stage if he likes the product or not and builds preferences based on favorable or unfavorable attitudes towards the brand. At the end of the affective stage the consumer develops a conviction of the usefulness of the purchase or in other words an intention to purchase the brand. In the conative phase the purchase or action is executed. Even though not included in most HOE models (Barry and Howard 1990; Smith et al. 2008; Vakratsas and Ambler 1999), consumer loyalty and advocacy ideally follows the action or purchase phase and represents a strong state of commitment to the brand. These stages have therefore been proposed as important additional parts by some (Mooradian et al. 2012; Riesenbeck and Perrey 2007).

Decisive for the sequence and flow of the single steps in the decision process is the involvement of consumers to the product or brand. According to Zaichkowsky (1985, p. 342), involvement is defined as "a person's perceived relevance of the object based on inherent needs, values, and interests," whereby objects refer to products or brands, and depends on situational factors. In respect to the decision-making process, involvement can influence the HOE in two ways (Assael 1987; Petty et al. 1983; Smith et al. 2008; Solomon 2011). First, depending on the level of involvement consumers need differing amounts of time to go through the phases (Lavidge and Steiner 1961). This means that for high involvement products like cars, consumers normally take longer when they for example search and process information and therefore need more time to get to the subsequent phase. Second, the level of involvement potentially also influences the sequence of the HOE stages (Barry and Howard 1990; Kotler and Keller 2010). With low involvement products the affective and conative phases could precede the cognitive phase as consumers do not "think" when buying the product but build attitudes after the purchase in the stage of using.

Consumers make countless decisions every day and are confronted with an overwhelming amount of information input (Mick et al. 2004). They therefore develop certain habits and "heuristics," which are shortcuts and "rules of thumb" used in decision making, to cope with this mental overload (Folkes 1988). Brands are the most common rule of thumb in the contemporary marketplace. They facilitate many purchase decisions and offer reassurance as they connect current and future decisions to experiences, satisfactions, and knowledge (Kapferer 2008; Keller 2008; Mooradian et al. 2012).

User-generated content and social media influence consumers in their purchase decision-making (Chen et al. 2011; cp. Kozinets et al. 2010). They therefore have to be seen as a marketing communication channels (Chen and Xie 2008). Brands as an integral part of consumers' decision-making are also impacted by content made public via social media platforms (Constantinides and Fountain 2008).

3 Research Setting

Applications like Facebook, Youtube, and many others have seen enormous growth in the past decade and have become a revolutionary trend influencing the way we use the Internet, communicate with others, and search for information. As consumers are becoming more familiar with advanced communication and media technologies, they now have to be recognized as active creators instead of passive, consuming participants (Kozinets, Hemetsberger and Schau 2008; Henderson and Bowley 2010). UGC represents the means for this participation and is usually referred to as the way in which people are active in social media (Kaplan and Haenlein 2010). User-generated environments created by UGC can be summarized as social media. In its various manifestations, social media constitutes the setting for this thesis – either directly, as two studies were conducted within social media applications, or indirectly, as social media served as the inspirational background of the studies.

To investigate the characteristics of UGBs, one study was directly conducted within the virtual world, Second Life. As part of the social media universe, virtual worlds are considered to lead the path to the future of the 3D Internet (de Mesa 2009; Hopkins 2009). Enabled by advances in 3D graphics, bandwidth and network connectivity, virtual worlds are computer-generated physical spaces, represented graphically in three dimensions, which can be experienced by many users, or so-called avatars, at once (Castronova 2005; Kohler et al. 2011; Mueller et al. 2011). Virtual worlds differ from other social media applications as they allow real time interactions, have avatars as fully customized virtual self-representations, and enable the exploration of the virtual environment in three dimensions (Kaplan and Haenlein 2009). In addition to that, virtual social worlds like SL function like real economies: they enable users to exchange services as well as virtual goods (Mennecke et al. 2009) and give users thereby the opportunity to create and capture the value of their efforts. Virtual social worlds put the user at the center of their business model as they rely almost exclusively on user-generated content (Bonsu and Darmody 2008). Virtual worlds present an ideal field to study the phenomenon of UGBs for various reasons: first, virtual worlds are spaces where users can freely and easily set up own businesses and build brands; second, SL as the most prominent example has produced several self-

Figure 2: Brand stores in Second Life

made real life millionaires (e.g. Anshe Chung for virtual real estate development) and allows many to live of their virtual activities; and third, the potential economic relevance of virtual good brands is supported by the growing market of virtual goods, which exceeded USD 7 billion in 2010 (In-Stat 2010). Virtual worlds furthermore illustrate the challenge for corporations to effectively employ social media for brand building, as a great number failed to establish value-adding and lasting presences.

The influences of social media marketing activities on brand attitudes were also studied within a social media application, as Facebook was used as an example to test the effects of consumers' commitment to the Facebook fanpage of a car manufacturer (see Figure 3). Users of the fanpage were thereby asked to participate in a survey to test for brand attitude effects. The other studies – an online experiment and an online survey – were conducted outside of the social media space, but were inspired by its influences on consumers and branding.

3 Research Setting 21

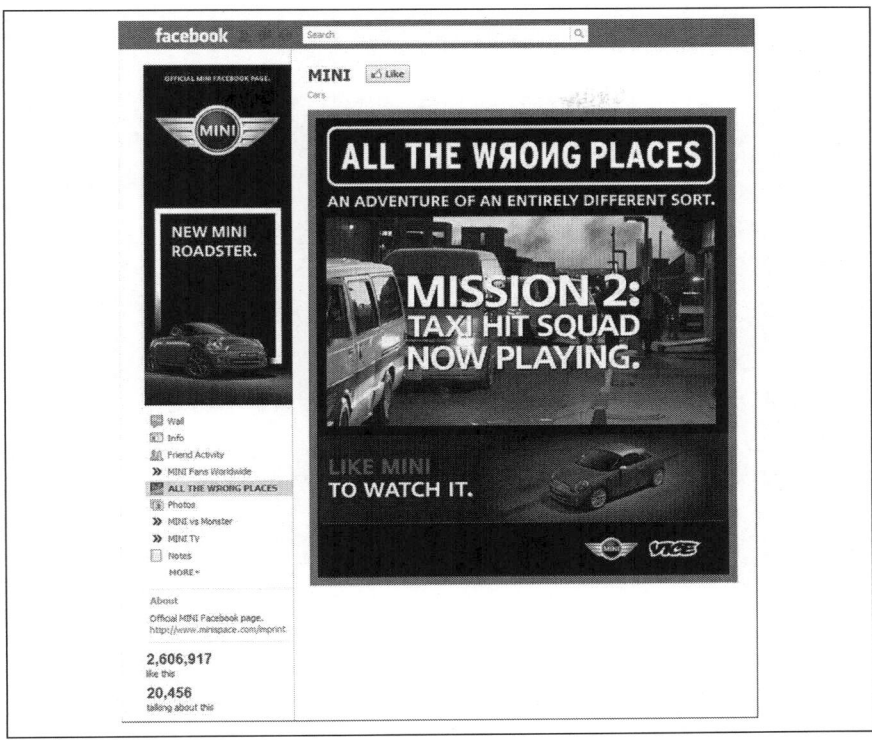

Figure 3: MINI Facebook Fanpage

4 Methodology

To gain a deeper understanding on the emergence and management of user-generated content and brands, their inherent utility and value for consumers, as well as on the effects of social media marketing for brands, a combination of qualitative and quantitative methods was used. This mix of methods was applied in order to employ the most appropriate techniques for the identified research questions.

Researchers developed the mixed method approach because of the limitations and caveats inherent in research methods. They felt that biases immanent in any single method could be neutralized by the biases of other methods. Mixed method approaches thereby use triangulation as a means to look for convergence across qualitative and quantitative methods (Tashakkori and Teddlie 1998). According to Creswell (2003):"A mixed method approach is one in which the researcher tends to base knowledge claims on pragmatic grounds (e.g., consequence-oriented, problem-centered, and pluralistic). It employs strategies of inquiry that involve collecting data either simultaneously or sequentially to best understand research problems. The data collection also involves gathering both numeric information (e.g., on instruments) as well as text information (e.g., on interviews) so that the final database represents both quantitative and qualitative information."

In mixing qualitative and quantitative methods, two different research paradigms are addressed. Whereas the quantitative approach applies a post-positivist claim for developing knowledge (i.e., cause and effect thinking; reduction to specific variables, hypotheses, and questions; use of measurement and observation; and the test of theories) and uses inquiries like experiments or surveys that yield statistical data, the qualitative approach emphasizes a constructivist perspective to develop knowledge (i.e., the multiple meanings of individual experiences, meanings socially and historically constructed, with an intent of developing a theory or pattern). Qualitative inquiries result in open-ended, emerging data with the primary intent of developing topics and themes from the data (Creswell 2003).

In comparison to single method approaches, mixed method approaches have several advantages: first, they enable the researcher to ask exploratory and confirmatory questions within a study and therefore theory generation and verifycation is possible within the same study (Tashakkori and Teddlie 1998); second, using multiple methods avoids over-reliance on a single method and thereby prevents method bias; and finally, by mixing methods, insights on different levels or units of analysis can be gained (Creswell 2003). As this dissertation project is dealing with consumers' perception, characteristics of user-generated brands and the overall impact of social media on brands and their perception, a mixed method approach is suitable as it allows studying different facets of the impact of user-generated content on branding.

Following this brief discussion of mixed method approaches, the single methods used within this dissertation project will be subsequently described in more detail.

4.1 Content Analysis Based on Qualitative Interviews

For our research project within the virtual world, Second Life, data collection included observation of activities, in-world participation, secondary analysis of various journals, newspapers and web pages, and qualitative interviews. A qualitative research approach was chosen as the exploration and understanding of the phenomenon was the goal (Creswell 2003; Denzin and Lincoln 1994). The semi-structured interviews were set up and conducted in accordance to suggestions on empirical social research (Flick 2009; Lincoln and Denzin 1994). They took place within the virtual world, Second Life, and were recorded, transcribed and anonymized. To analyze the gathered content, open coding typical for grounded theory was applied (Glaser and Strauss 1967). As an inductive investigative process, the grounded theory method seeks to formulate a theory about a phenomenon by systematically gathering and analyzing relevant data. Content analysis was focused on object-linguistic and metaphysical codes typifying the characteristics of the brands under investigation. In order to ensure inter-coder reliability, two researchers continuously negotiated the meanings of codes and the identified characteristics. In this way relevant themes regarding the research question could be identified, compared, and cross-checked in observation of the relevant brands in Second Life and other secondary data.

4.2 Experiment

For the study on the perception of user-generated brands, an experimental research design in combination with an online survey was chosen. Experiments allow the researcher to control the research situation so that causal relationships between different variables can be evaluated (Zikmund 2003). Sample survey designs in contrast are insufficient in explaining the causes of an effect or relationship (Sarris and Reiß 2005). The experimental type used for this thesis was a one-factor, between-subjects design in an online environment. The online experiment itself can be described as a new class of experiments as it does not fulfill the settings of a field or laboratory experiment (Sarris and Reiß 2005). This type of experiment was chosen as it allows for greater reachability of test persons and provides higher external validity. To counteract the disadvantages we controlled for confounding variables by employing a large randomized sample, recruited participants from various sources (social network sites, banners on websites, mailing lists, etc.), and designed the experiment to minimize dropouts (Welker et al. 2005).

4.3 Structural Equation Modeling Based on Online Survey Data

In addition to exploratively describing UGBs and quantitatively analyzing their perceived value for consumers with an experiment, online surveys were conducted to statistically investigate the perceived value of brands' social dimension and the effects of social media activities on the purchase decision-making process. The relationships between the constructs of the developed, theoretical models were tested with multivariate data analyses, i.e., structural equation modeling (SEM) (Bagozzi and Yi 1988; Bentler and Bonnett 1980; Fornell and Larcker 1981). SEM allows the researcher to simultaneously examine a series of interrelated dependence relationships among the measured variables and latent constructs as well as between several latent constructs (Hair et al. 1998).

This mix of qualitative and quantitative methods represents a holistic approach to answering the research questions. This methodological approach was chosen as it helps to compensate for disadvantages that the application of certain single methods has and yields the possibility for falsification (i.e., divergent findings) as well as stronger inference and reliability of the results (Creswell 2003; Tashakkori and Teddlie 1998).

After describing the thematic, theoretical, and methodological foundations of this thesis, the following section, Part B, will introduce the individual studies composing this thesis in more detail, before theoretical and managerial implications as well as limitations and future research directions are discussed.

Part B –
Articles Contributing to this Doctoral Thesis

5 Overview of Papers Included in Doctoral Thesis

This cumulative dissertation consists of a number of published and unpublished papers either in conference proceedings or journals and follows the standards for cumulative dissertations at the University of Innsbruck – School of Management. According to these standards, a minimum of three articles fulfilling the quality standards of international, refereed journals is required. At least one of these papers needs to be single authored.

Evaluation: Each single authored unpublished paper counts as 1 point. The amount of points attributed to published papers depends on the ranking of the publication outlet according to the VHB (Verband der Hochschullehrer für Betriebswirtschaft) ranking or the Social Sciences Citation Index (SSCI) impact factor at the time of publication: A and A+ journals are attributed 3 points; B journals are attributed 2 points, and C journals as well as double blind reviewed full conference papers are attributed 1 point. In the case of articles with multiple authors, the amount of points that are attributed to a publication outlet is multiplied by $3/(n+2)$, n being the number of authors of the article.

Please consult table 1 for an overview on the points attributable to each publication included in this dissertation.

5.1 Paper 1: User-generated Brands Emerging from Social Media: What Corporate Brands can Learn from Brand Management in Virtual Worlds

The emergence of social media and consumers' increased time online presents opportunities and challenges for brand management. While large brands are still struggling to get a grip on their social media efforts, individual users have demonstrated that creating brands within these user-generated online environments is doable. This article introduces the idea of user-generated brands. User-generated brands are created, originally unintentionally, by individual users or communities of users outside of their professional routines in social media environments, where their products are publicly available and show an effort of creativity. Grounded in brand management theory, we use qualitative data to explore the characteristics, processes, and particularities of this emerging phenomenon that can be witnessed within the virtual world of Second Life. The results show that user-generated brands and brand management in SL exhibit specific characteristics and that being open, encouraging participation and maintaining authenticity are essential strategies to brands in this marketplace.

5.2 Paper 2: Perception of User-generated Brands: A New Power in the Minds of Consumers?

Consumers do not only have an increasing influence on brands, they even create brands themselves. The existence of brands created by users suggests that those brands exhibit additional value to consumers that differentiates them from large commercial brands. This study therefore investigates the value of user-generated brands from a consumer perspective. With an experiment conducted with 804 participants we demonstrate that the origin of a brand has an influence on consumers' perception of sympathy, authenticity, and credibility. The results point to a value-adding utility of user-created brands, which distinguishes them from commercial brands and could offer a competitive advantage.

5.3 Paper 3: The Value-enhancing Role of Social Networks Around Brands: The Concept of Social Brand Value

Prevalent branding concepts need to catch up with the reality of the social media revolution and the emergence of communities, social networks, and user-generated content portals. Given the importance of social interactions in the new media environment, there is an emerging need to account for social value in marketing and branding. Based on social capital theory, we introduce the concept of social brand value (SBV), defined as the perceived value derived by exchange and interactions with other users of the brand. A quantitative study with 1,301 participants is used to demonstrate the influence that the social brand value construct has for consumers' brand evangelism and willingness to pay a price premium. Our findings show that brands such as Apple, Coke, and Microsoft differ in their social brand value and that SBV has a significant impact on the investigated variables. Further, SBV also mediates the effect between quality on the one side and willingness to pay a price premium as well as brand evangelism on the other side.

5.4 Paper 4: The Impact of Social Media on Brand Awareness and Purchase Intention: The Case of MINI on Facebook

In this article, we analyze how social media activities in specific the Facebook page of a car producer affect the perception of brands and ultimately influence consumers' purchase decision. Based on an online survey with users of the corporations Facebook fanpage, and in accordance to hierarchy of effects theory, our findings show the positive effect fanpage engagement on consumers' brand awareness, word-of-mouth (WOM) activities, and purchase intention. The findings further indicate that annoyance with the fanpage due to information overload leads to negative effects on fanpage commitment and to decreased WOM activities. From a theoretical standpoint the results of this study contribute to our understanding of the value-enhancing potential of social media campaigns.

6 User-generated Brands: What Corporate Brands Can Learn from Brand Management in Virtual Worlds

6.1 Introduction

Firms are facing a new communication reality that has been created by the rise of social media applications. Concurrently branding and brand management has become a key marketing priority for most companies (Aaker and Joachimsthaler, 2000, Keller, 2009). Yet, there is little knowledge and consensus on how brands and branding can or should be developed in the modern interactive marketplace (Naylor et al., 2012, Chen et al., 2011, Kozinets et al., 2010, Keller, 2009). For the management of brands, these new developments in the way people communicate with each other present both opportunities and challenges (Keller and Richey, 2006, Mueller et al., 2011). With consumers spending more and more time on platforms such as Facebook, Youtube or Twitter, an increasing share of the interaction with and the experience around brands occurs within these new communication environments. Because content in these social media environments is created and co-created by users interactively, individuals and communities increasingly have the power to influence existing brands (OECD, 2007, Kane et al., 2009, Holt, 2002, Hoffman and Novak, 2009) or even to perpetuate already abandoned brands (Muniz and Schau 2007; Muniz and Schau 2005). Consumption of information in the contemporary space of social media networks becomes inseparable from production, which leads to new levels of user information, innovation and creativity (Kozinets et al., 2008). Taken together, a new dimension to branding and marketing communications is added, which is going to change the way brands communicate and interact with their customers (Engagementdb, 2009, Kaplan and Haenlein, 2010, Keller, 2009, Klaassen, 2006, Court et al., 2006).

While large brands are still struggling to get a grip on their social media efforts, users in social media environments have shown that creating and establishing successful brands is possible (Füller and Von Hippel, 2008, Füller et al., 2007, Cova and White, 2010). For instance, consider the cases of Apache or Linux, where brands were co-created by a community of users.

With this study we seek to identify popular brands that emerged from users' initiatives and we aim to shed light on their unique characteristics in relation to existing corporate brand characteristics. To tackle this research task, we label brands that originated from single users or a group of users through user-generated content, rather than companies, as user-generated brands (UGB). We study the social media environment of Second Life (SL), where the existence of user-generated brands created by individuals is most visible, because in this virtual social world users are free to create, own and sell their content (de Mesa, 2009, la Ferla, 2009). We first outline the underlying theoretic brand foundations and discuss the changed nature of branding in social media environments. Next we take an affordances perspective to highlight the particularities of branding in virtual worlds. Our empiric study then identifies the existence and characteristics of UGBs before we conclude with what brands can learn from UGBs.

6.2 Theoretical Foundations

6.2.1 Definition and Core Characteristics of Brands

Branding and brand management has conventionally been envisaged from the organizational standpoint that a company has possession of its brand and unilaterally establishes its positioning (Keller, 1993). Today marketing theory has moved beyond this view and widely accepted a co-creation process for establishing brands (Vargo and Lusch 2004; Payne et al. 2009; Mühlbacher and Hemetsberger 2008; Diamond et al. 2009). With the new communication possibilities offered by social media the co-creation and open source aspect of branding has gained even more importance (Pitt et al., 2006, Kozinets et al., 2008).

In accordance with the American Marketing Association a brand is a 'name, term, sign, symbol, or design, or a combination of them intended to identify the goods and services of one seller or group of sellers and to differentiate them from those of competition' (Kotler, 1997). In real world marketing practice, however, a brand refers to a name or symbol that has created a certain amount of awareness, reputation and prominence in the marketplace (Keller, 2008). Today brands are widely described as complex entities and value systems as they entail knowledge and meaning (Keller 2008; Kapferer 2008; de Chernatony and Riley 1998; Muniz and O'Guinn 2001; Diamond et al. 2009; Vargo and Lusch 2011). This meaning is co-created in the interplay between the brand as a material object, the social actors engaged with it and interactions happening around it (e.g. in consumer collectives) (Vargo and Lusch, 2004, Mühlbacher and Hemetsberger, 2008, Elliott, 1994, Schau et al., 2009). Brands are therefore no longer static outcomes of marketing managers' actions but are rather perceived as dynamic entities, actively contributing to the lives of consumers (Fournier, 1998, Merz et al., 2009).

To describe a brand more precisely the definition of a brand alone is insufficient and more detailing characteristics of brands have to be outlined. A comprehensive list of attributes shared by strong brands was summarized by Keller[1] (2000, cp. Riesenbeck and Perrey, 2007, Hollis, 2008, Aaker and Joachimsthaler, 2000): First, they are excellent in delivering the benefits customers want and they listen to and act on the comments customers have. Second, strong brands stay relevant by providing innovative products of highest quality and adapting intangibles like imagery and brand personality to consumers needs. Third, strong brands are properly positioned as they occupy particular niches in consumers' minds and differentiate themselves from competitors. Fourth, they are consistent in the core associations and images they communicate. Fifth, they coordinate their marketing communication to send a consistent message across all the elements supporting a brand, including advertising. Six, it is important for strong brands to understand what the brand means to consumers.

Social media has altered the way companies and brands can communicate their messages to consumers. Applications like Facebook, Youtube and many others have seen enormous growth in the past decade and have become a revolutionary trend influencing our communication habits. As consumers are becoming more familiar with advanced communication and media technologies, they now have to be recognized as active creators instead of passive, consuming participants (Kozinets, Hemetsberger and Schau 2008; Henderson and Bowley 2010). User-generated content (UGC, also called user-created content or user-generated media) represents the means for this participation and is usually referred to as the way in which people are active in social media (Kaplan and Haenlein, 2010). The term is usually applied to describe the various forms of media content that is online, publicly available and created by end-users in an creative effort outside of professional routines (OECD, 2007). The user-generated environments created by this kind of content can be summarized as social media. This is in line with Kaplan and Haenlein (2010) who define social media as "a group of Internet-based applications that build on the ideological and technological foundations of

---

[1] For the purpose of our research we focus only on the six most relevant attributes (out of a total of ten).

Web 2.0, and that allow the creation and exchange of User Generated Content" (Kaplan and Haenlein, 2010, Smith, 2009, Kim et al., 2009). According to this definition, social media covers many internet-based applications, including blogs, social networking sites, content communities, virtual game worlds and virtual social worlds.

With the advances of the user-generated environments of social media and increasing brand interactions taking place within these realms, brands become more open to the influences of consumers (Pitt et al. 2006; Payne et al. 2009; Kates 2004; Kozinets et al. 2010; Kozinets, Hemetsberger and Schau 2008). In the next section we argue that consumers influence is leading to the emerging phenomenon of UGB.

6.2.2 User-generated Brands

Prior research has shown that user-generated content and co-creative influences of consumers have value enhancing effects for brands. According to Cova (1997), the tribalization of consumption effects consumers in the postmodern era to value products not only for their utility value, but for their linking value, enabled by co-creating activities of these tribes. Furthermore, Muniz and O'Guinn (2001) demonstrated that activities in brand communities clearly affect the value of a brand for community members (cp. Jang et al., 2008). Similarly, Schau et al. (2009) propose a process of user-driven collective value creation within brand communities, which manifests itself in several practices: evangelizing, justifying, welcoming, empathizing, governing, documenting, badging, milestoning, staking, customizing, grooming and commoditizing. Thematically aggregated in the four functions of impression management, social networking, community engagement and brand use, these practices realize brand value for consumers beyond influences of a firm or marketer. Muniz and Schau (2007, 2005) argue further that co-creation of brand communities in social media environments can even perpetuate abandoned brands by creating valuable brand content.

Recent findings go beyond the influencing role that users have on brands. Supported by findings on user innovation and users' entrepreneurial activities (von Hippel, 2005, Shah and Tripsas, 2007), the notion that businesses and brands can be established from user-generated content is gaining traction. Füller et al. (2007) found that online-communities of users who share a specific interest were channeling their creativity to design, produce, share and consume customized products within their group of fellow enthusiasts and were thereby building meaningful and enchanting brands. Another relevant research stream revolves around Shah and Tripsas work (2007, Shah and Smith, 2010), who introduced the notion of user innovators creating their own business and discussed how they become "accidental" entrepreneurs by having a product idea through own use and sharing it with others. Building on these early findings and a recent definition by von Hippel et al. (2011), we define user-generated brands as brands, which are created from user-generated content – originally unintended – by single users or a group of users. They emerge through social user interaction around a certain topic of natural interest. Usually, UGBs emerge and are formed around the natural activities and behaviors of users that start to label their created goods (tangible as well as intangible). At least in the beginning, no commercial purposes are followed with these grassroots brands. Users consider brand building activities not as a job, but as part of their pastime and an intrinsically rewarding activity. The creation of a brand can therefore be described as unintended at the outset, i.e. happening "accidentally".

Looking at virtual worlds, users have shown that creating successful brands is doable and frequently their initiatives have outperformed established corporations (de Mesa, 2009).

6.2.3 Affordances of Virtual Worlds for User-generated Brands

We try to capture the particularities of virtual worlds by using the term "affordances". Gibson (Gibson, 1979) introduced the idea of affordances to explain how people orient to the objects in their world in terms of the possibilities the objects afford for action. According to an affordance perspective materiality of an object factors, shapes, or invites and at the same time constraints a set of specific uses (Zammuto 2007). Particular affordances of an object may be different for different species (Gibson, 1979) and depend on the intent of actors enacting them (Boureau and Robey 2005). Hence, a technology needs to be referenced to the social setting or in the words of Zammuto et al. (2007, p.753) "it makes limited sense to talk about a door handle without discussing the people opening the open doors". We use an affordance lens to describe virtual world's affordances as actionable properties between the world and an actor (Norman, 2004). This helps to understand the relationship between the technology of virtual worlds and social actions that are possible to do within them (Hutchby, 2001, Jones and Karsten, 2008, Hemp, 2006).

Virtual worlds offer unique affordances that provide a space for the emergence of user-generated brands. Virtual worlds are computer-generated physical spaces, represented graphically in three dimensions, which can be experienced by many users, or so-called avatars, at once (Castronova, 2005, Mueller et al., 2011, Hemp, 2006, DMD et al., 2007). As part of the social media universe, virtual worlds are considered to lead the path to the future of the 3D internet (Hopkins, 2009, de Mesa, 2009). Their affordances are the result of the confluence of advances in 3D graphics, bandwidth and network connectivity. We will discuss the affordances that foster user-generated brands, namely the ability to create content, user embodiment, three-dimensionality and real time interactions.

One of virtual worlds' key affordances that allows users to create their own brands is the ability to create content and products, as virtual worlds rely almost exclusively on user-generated content (Bonsu and Darmody, 2008). Second Life for instance provides its residents with the equivalent of atoms – small elements of virtual matter called 'prims' – so that they can build anything they imagine from scratch (Ondrejka, 2004). Scripting or programming allows content creators to add behaviors and interactivity to objects inside Second Life, thanks to the embedded programming language. Second Life's total commitment to user-generated content combined with the inception of property rights turns Second Life into an infinitely scalable content creator's dream and an engine of creation (Hof 2006, Ondrejka 2007). These mechanisms have turned virtual worlds into a level playing field between users and companies. In the past establishing strong brands was the monopoly of selected companies, because branding entailed substantial resources. The advent of user-generated content is democratizing branding. Similarly to the democratization of innovation (von Hippel 2005), where users are increasingly able to innovate for themselves, user-generated environments are allowing participants to build their on brands. The head start of established corporations in terms of infrastructure, established distribution channels or advertising budget is of little relevance in a world that is built upon creativity and user engagement.

Virtual worlds not only allow anyone to create anything they can imagine, but also look like anyone they want to be. This affordance of user embodiment, makes avatars fully customizable virtual self-representations, where individuals can alter their avatars along multiple dimensions, including appearance, clothing, accessories, and possessions. The self-expression is unconstraint by scarce resources (la Ferla, 2009). Both in the physical and virtual world, part of the value that brands deliver steams from supporting personal identity formation (Ahuvia 2005, Belk 1988). Consumers tend to prefer brands that match their own characteristics (Aaker 2004). What is unique about virtual worlds is that now everyone has access to the tools to create their idealized self-representation. While creating self-made products is a resource intense process in the physical world, in the world of bits and bytes less resources are required. The prominent users of virtual worlds thrive by their imagination, intrinsic motivation and deep understanding of user behavior.

User embodiment in combination with the affordance to explore the virtual environment in three dimensions can provide the user with a deeper understanding of the functionality of the experienced product or service and allows for richer representations of products as compared to other internet-based media used for the same purposes (Sawhney et al., 2005).

Finally, virtual worlds afford real time interactions, which facilitates enhanced communication and collaboration. Besides various forms of asynchronous communication, users may communicate in real-time using voice or text chat to share and discuss their creations with other users. Besides the value of a product itself, the interaction with others contributes to the strength of a brand (Keller and Lehmann, 2003). The close ties that users have in a social virtual world gives users an edge over corporate ventures, which enter the virtual world as novices.

Summarizing the affordances of virtual worlds, one can conclude that virtual worlds turn into real economies: They enable users to exchange services as well as virtual goods (DMD et al., 2007, Mennecke et al., 2009) and give users the opportunity to create and capture the value of their efforts. This has turned virtual worlds into spaces where users can freely and easily set up own businesses and build brands. SL as the most prominent virtual world has produced several self-made real life millionaires (e.g. Anshe Chung) and allows many to live of their virtual activities. The potential economic relevance of virtual good brands is supported by the growing market of virtual goods, which exceeded USD 7 billion in 2010 (In-Stat, 2010).

While the unique affordances of virtual worlds enable participants to create their own brands, corporations struggle to effectively employ virtual worlds for brand building. A great number of established brands from Adidas to Xerox started to engage in various social media applications and had established presences in virtual worlds – with mixed results (Hassouneh and Brengman, 2011, Arakji and Lang, 2008, de Mesa, 2009, Kaplan and Haenlein, 2010). Hopes were to use SL for marketing purposes and to profit from the innovative and creative potential of the users (Kohler et al., 2011). In mid 2007 around 150 real life companies were observed to be active in SL. By mid 2010, more than eighty percent of those companies had left SL. The dropout of corporate brands can mostly be attributed to their failure to offer additional value to the users and their missing understanding of and connection to SL users.

In contrast to the failures of real life companies in SL, grassroots brands created by users have been successful in sustaining a profitable business, which provides real life subsistence for the owners in many cases (MacMillan, 2007, Gardiner, 2007). SL brands like Stilletto Moody, Vista Animations, GothiCatz or RGF Estate have proven over the past years that building and sustaining a successful brand is achievable. How are users of virtual worlds building their brands? Why are they experiencing increased prominence? How do they leverage virtual worlds affordances? In our empirical study, we analyze UGB's relevance and shed light on their brand building process in order to understand the factors that are crucial for brands in user-generated environments.

6.3 Empirical Study

6.3.1 Research Method

To explore this emerging phenomenon of brands created by users as opposed to companies, the empirical research followed an inductive investigative process consisting of multiple case studies that were designed to illuminate the existence and nature of UGB's and gain insights on the mechanisms of branding and brand management in SL. Case studies as a research strategy allow to investigate and describe an emerging phenomenon in its context and to develop a respective theory (Yin, 2009). We used multiple case studies to be able to identify common patterns or characteristics across the cases of UGBs in order to develop the foundation for a theory on UGBs and branding in a virtual worlds environment (Yin, 2009, Stake, 1995).

Collection of the data included participant observation in SL by the authors, documentation like blog and discussion forum entries and interviews with users, brand owners and Linden Lab experts. To increase the trustworthiness of the case studies, we relied on these various sources of data. Our derived theoretical principles are based and evidenced on patterns immanent across the investigated cases. To ensure reliability (Yin, 2009), we documented the single steps of our research program in an online protocol tool, which was shared among the researchers and also used to coordinate the efforts.

To identify the most relevant and most successful brands in SL we used a two-step approach. First, we looked at brand specific blogs and other brand related communication among users, engaged in discussions on the SL commerce forums and used an online survey (100 respondents) to compile a long list of popular brands in SL. We asked participants about the most popular and successful brands in SL and inquired about the drivers of success for these popular brands were. Whereas the participants for the survey were randomly chosen SL users, the participants in the discussion forum voluntarily took part in the discussion about brands in SL, which we triggered deliberately. Second, we identified a list of 25 brands (commercial and non-commercial) based on the frequency of mentions in the survey and on the discussion forums. This list was then reviewed with managers at Linden Lab, the creators of SL and the experts overlooking commercial activities in SL. During the interviews we cross-checked our list of brands with the user-generated brand owners. As the landscape of businesses in SL is rather fragmented and commercial data on brands in SL was not available, it was important to get the input from users, brand owners as well as Linden Lab experts to identify examples of insightful brands for the case studies. This input was then used to condense the initial list and compile a final list of 20 of the most popular brands in SL (see Table 2). Next, we conducted a series of semi-structured interviews (n = 12) with the owners or managers of brands in SL from our list, who were willing to be interviewed. The respondents' age ranged from 28 to 50 (Avg. 39) and female participants accounted for 60% of the sample. 75% of the sample indicated that they could live on their earnings from their virtual business (see Table 1). The interviews were conducted directly within SL and lasted on average around one hour.

The content of the collected data was analyzed using open coding typical of a grounded theory approach (Glaser and Strauss, 1967). The process of consensus-building thereby had two steps as the researchers first independently coded, analyzed and interpreted the data and then discussed the results jointly in several face-to-face sessions to arrive at a shared understanding and consent concerning analysis and interpretation. In the first step of analysis, we placed conceptual labels on responses that described discrete events, experiences, and feelings reported in the interviews. After initial reading and noting specific themes in the data, three researchers, two of which fulfilled the requirement of not being biased by preconceived ideas, coded the data set independently. Next, we engaged in an independent process of axial coding to identify common patterns and connections between the three sets of codings. In order to reduce individual coding biases, we corrected synonyms in several team sessions by negotiating meanings and checking with the primary texts. Hence, a one-sided interpretation of the data was avoided and the validity of the results were enhanced (Maxwell, 2008). In the second step, consensus about the interpretations of the data was

Table 2: Details of the participants of the study

Participant Number	Alias	Start point of SL Business (Year)	Initial monetary investment (USD)	Ability to live of SL earnings	Age	Gender
1	Scarlett	2005	20	yes	–	female
2	Lyle	2007	40	yes	34	male
3	Thora	2005	300	yes	50	female
4	Kaitlyn	2007	10	yes	29	female
5	Eli	2005	0	yes	42	female
6	Matilda	2008	5	partially	45	–
7	Scott	2007	0	yes	35	male
8	Janean	2009	30	no	28	female
9	Eve	2009	1000	no	50	female
10	Freddy	2006	0	yes	38	male
11	Ross	2006	1500	yes	39	male
12	Clarine	2007	100	yes	35	female

formed through several rounds of joint discussions and iterative referrals to the literature and research in related areas. We thereby also ensured that each factor or theme appeared in the data repeatedly to achieve concept saturation (Strauss and Corbin, 1990, Glaser and Strauss, 1967). The final coding scheme can be found in Appendix B. The following results focus on the identified concepts that are most relevant to the purpose of the study and that stretched across the major part of the interviews. The results are structured to describe the observed UGBs, their genesis and their defining characteristics.

6.3.2 Results

The brands under investigation represent various industries typical for the business landscape in SL (including fashion, animations, vending systems, real estate, etc.). Of those brands, three will be shortly introduced representatively: One of the most prominent examples for fashion brands in SL is GothiCatz. The brand focuses on a unique style of fashion for female and male avatars. It is considered to be a "phenomenon" in SL and is known for starting new trends. Vista Animations is one of the leading players in the animations business focusing on

6.3 Empirical Study

Table 3: Defining attributes for UGBs with describing comments

Category	Attributes	Exemplary Quotes	Source
Genesis/ Establishment	No initial commercial intention	As you can tell, I didn't come to SL to make money	Eli
	Start through fun and curiosity	I created my account on Second Life just to explore, pure curiosity. But then I realized there was a possibility to work my creativity there.	Clarine
	Unintended creation of business	Actually [starting a business] was a mistake because I was making for me and put on sale just to try, not really having the intention to start a business like I have now	Kaitlyn
	Word-of-mouth promotion	Personally, word-of-mouth [is essential for promotion] … 'Build a better mousetrap and the world will beat a path to your door'. We've never really advertised, nor do I see the need to. Show, don't tell, what your strengths are.	Freddy
Process of brand origination	Embeddedness in community	We love our customers and many ideas for innovation come from listening to them	Freddy
	Focus on interactivity	For me the most important thing since I started my business is the communication to customers	Clarine
	Authenticity	The [corporate] brands failed to deliver products consumed in sl ... Companies who succeed in sl are selling sl	Clarine
	Collective creative process	it was mostly a group of individuals that encouraged and inspired each other while creating things by themselves	Eli

animations for SL avatars and has already expanded into other virtual worlds. With RGF Estates, one of the leading real estate businesses in SL was also part of our investigation. RGF Estates sells and rents virtual land in the SL grid and also operates the school "learnavatar" where new users in SL are introduced to the virtual reality. Users and owners were referring to the respective businesses as being brands mainly because of their popularity in the community and the high level of product recognition among users. These brands represent typical examples of UGBs. In the following we will describe defining attributes and the origin process of those brands (see also Table 3).

Genesis of user-generated brands: When the creators of the observed brands were asked to share their story of how they started their brand, notably across the spectrum all of them entered SL out of curiosity, leisure or fun. Not one of them was driven by commercial reasons at the outset. This means that none of the interviewed founders started using SL out of commercial intentions or motivation. As they were exploring the new environment, they started creating their own products because of two main reasons. First, when users weren't finding the products they wanted, they took matters into their own hands. Products were either not of the quality the users would have liked them to be or were simply non-existent at that time. Two such examples were Matilda and Scarlett who could not find what they wanted when they started engaging in SL and therefore started to create their own products:

> Matilda: "I couldn't find what I wanted, out of frustration I figured I could do better, so learned what I needed to make the product that I wanted. I had no money, couldn't afford to put anything at all into SL."

> Scarlett: "I went skin shopping and discovered that none of the skins available at that time appealed to me. I decided to make my own skin for personal use."

Second, users' creative efforts were simply driven by the desire and curiosity to engage in the creative play of the virtual world. SL gives its' users the unique possibility to easily be creative and get into contact with peers who have the same desire. When Thora, a fashion designer, startet in SL, she was fascinated about SL and the creative opportunities it offered:

> Thora: "[SL offers] an incredible opportunity to meet like-minded individuals … Immediately [I] came into contact with all kind of creatives. … And very early on saw other artists developing clothing here … [after meeting other designers] I started to develop [clothing]."

The step from creating own products for own use or out of interest to actually selling the product and starting an own business was generally unplanned, a single initiative and happened "accidentally" in all observed cases. Some of the owners were "pushed" by other avatars into selling their products when they saw and wanted to have some of the self-made products. Other owners were starting a shop as their products were complimented and they were interested to see if they would sell. So even though they never wanted to start a commercial business when entering SL, they unexpectedly found themselves selling more and more of their products, to the point where they had a flourishing business.

Talking about the start of their SL business, Kaitlyn and Scarlett illustrate this point.

> Kaitlyn: "Actually [starting a business] was a "mistake" because I was making for me and put on sale just to try, not really having the intention to start a business like I have now."

> Scarlett: "While wearing my skin around SL I got constant [messages] from strangers about where the skins could be purchased. When I'd tell them I'd made the skins myself I was offered tons of lindens for copies of them so [I] decided to open [a] shop."

Ironically the creation of products was more associated with play rather than work. The joy of being creative and developing own products was the main driving force of these entrepreneurs in SL. The commercial aspect of their creative work was something that came into play only later. Eli for example pointed this out:

> Eli: "I was playing, then suddenly I was selling, then suddenly I had a couple of fad items ... As you can tell, I didn't come to SL to make money. It just happened."

User-generated brand creation process: For establishing their brand, the creators of the observed UGBs didn't use any kind of advertising to promote their brand. Instead they were relying solely on word-of-mouth promotion by their customers. To spur and influence the word-of-mouth among users, they put the focus on product quality and constant innovation as a mean of promotion instead of advertising. If users like a product or a brand in SL, news about this product or brand can quickly go viral. The quotes from Clarine and Freddy are typical for the attitudes of SL brand owners when it comes to promotion: Offer a better product than your competitors and consumers will come on their own.

> Clarine: "There were maybe 2 months in 2008 I invested money advertising ..., and then I never advertised again. I don't participate on events, fashion shows, promotions, hunts, sponsorships; don't advertise on magazines, anywhere. [My] store is one of the most popular and recognized [brands] in second life though. ... It's like a chain reaction, I send a notice [to the community] announcing a new release and they come to buy and teleport all their friends."

> Freddy: "Personally, word-of-mouth [is essential for promotion] ... 'Build a better mousetrap and the world will beat a path to your door'. We've never really advertised, nor do I see the need to. Show, don't tell, what your strengths are."

Once established, UGBs share a set of common characteristics that makes them identifiable. First, the role of customers to UGBs has various unique aspects. Besides them being the purchasers of the products, they are a source of inspiration for innovation and actively co-create the brand through interaction with the creator and other consumers, feedback, word-of-mouth and by establishing brand communities. UGBs are deeply embedded in the community of users and customers and therefore their influence on what the brand does and what it stands for is strong. When asked about the role of consumers in building their brand, Freddy and Clarine pointed out the role of customers as a source of inspiration, encouragement and ongoing feedback:

> Freddy: "We love our customers and many ideas for innovation come from listening to them. But one needs to be selective – out of every 100 suggestions we get, only about 2 are of merit. The art is knowing which is which."
>
> Clarine: "For me the most important thing since I started my business is the communication to customers ... My customers encourage me a lot, I'm so grateful for their constant feedback and support."

The second unique characteristic of UGBs is the collective creative process in product development. UGB creators not only get feedback and ideas from customers, but the creative exchange among users is an important source of creativity (Chesney et al., 2009). Innovation thereby doesn't necessarily come from individuals, but is the product of a collective effort, which makes use of the abundant innovative resources available in an environment like SL. The passage by Eli demonstrates this:

> Eli: "I think the group [of users] inspired me to actually put things out to sell, and we bounced ideas off of each other .... But it was mostly a group of individuals that encouraged and inspired each other while creating things by themselves."

Third, authenticity, uniqueness, quality and innovation are among the most important images customers in SL are looking for. To deliver on those, UGBs have to understand what customers want and have to strive to always offer the best and most innovative products in their market. It is not enough to jump on an existing trend or niche, but becoming successful means taking control, being innovative and shaping the market. One brand creator described the trend shaping role of his brand:

> Clarine: "[My] brand really starts trends in Second Life and it's considered a phenomena."

One of the mistakes corporate brands were making in SL was their lack of striving for excellence in SL. As UGBs were constantly creating authentic new designs, features and more realism in their products, the efforts of corporate brands soon failed to capture the interests of users. UGBs live up to the expectations and desires users have of products in SL and give them something unique and tailored that they can identify with. Asked about how she came up with product ideas, Eli mentioned the following:

> Eli: "I saw that certain things were wanted by customers, I gave them what they wanted and tried to add in as many cute tricks to the items as I could."

Through the effort of meeting the expectations of SL user and delivering to their needs UGBs create meaning and value for customers in SL. Nevertheless, it is not through effort alone that this core brand creating process works, it is rather the understanding of the environment and its users and the knowledge and feeling of how to cater to their needs that creates meaningful brands.

6.4 Discussion

Taking an affordances perspective, we introduced the phenomenon of user-generated brands. As Zammuto (2007) points out, there can be no affordance absent actor intent. While among the majority of corporate brands the traditional understanding of strong brands is still prevalent (Keller, 2000), UGB demonstrate that the affordances of virtual worlds present opportunities for new forms of creating and managing brands.

Are the ventures created by residents of virtual worlds indeed brands? Recalling that a brand is a marker of differentiation and identification (Kotler, 1997) and is defined by its awareness, reputation and prominence in the marketplace (Keller, 2008), we find considerable evidence that the studied instances within virtual worlds are indeed brands for two main reasons: First, the analyzed cases use proprietary names and symbols, which most of the brand creators have registered, to mark their products. Second, our investigations into the virtual market of SL demonstrate that the entrepreneurs and their creations are widely recognized in the SL marketplace. The selection process to identify the relevant brands was designed to capture the brands in the marketplace SL that meet the criteria of awareness, reputation and prominence as we asked consumers to point out their most popular brands.

The affordances of virtual worlds create new opportunities for entrepreneurship and brand building that UGBs explore and utilize comprehensively. In comparing UGBs to the traditional understanding of strong brands, one key difference stands out: UGBs embrace the co-creating aspect of brand management to an unprecedented level as their brand and its meaning are constantly co-created and shaped by its users. The content creation affordance of virtual worlds therefore has several implications. One of the notable differences is the fun and curiosity aspect of getting into product development and the accidental nature of the entrepreneurship (Shah and Tripsas, 2007). The entrepreneurial logic found among the brand creators can be described by what Read et al have described as effectual (Read et al., 2009). Not one of the participants in our study started their business out of predictive rationality. They rather accidentally found a market niche and began to actively shape it. Another major difference in the genesis lies with the communication and advertising strategy. Whereas real life commercial brands still rely heavily on advertising to communicate their message consistently to consumers (Keller, 2008), UGBs rather let the products speak for themselves and let the customers and users spread the word. Word-of-mouth is essential for promoting and can take the form of direct interactions between users or indirect communication via blogs or via other social media applications. Word-of-mouth promotion in general has been long acknowledged to play an important role in shaping consumers' attitudes and behaviors (Brown and Reingen, 1987). The accessibility, reach, and transparency, social media applications are offering today is empowering this form of marketing as never before (Kozinets et al., 2010). UGBs therefore heavily rely on users' word-of-mouth activities as no classical marketing or advertising is used and let thereby users take partial control over their brands (cp. Cova and Pace, 2006, Holt, 2004).

The three main differentiating characteristics of UGBs in comparison with corporate brands, which are driven by the affordances of virtual worlds and user generated content, are embeddedness in community, collective creative effort and authenticity of brand image. First, UGBs make interaction with customers, who are effectively also co-users, the core principle of their business. As users created them, UGBs show a better understanding of consumers' needs and desires because of their user-background. Following Cova and Cova (2002, Cova et al., 2007) the network of SL users can be described as a tribe of consumers linked by shared experience, passion or emotion around the virtual environment. Out of this tribe single users emerge to build a UGB. Those individuals actively engage the tribe in brand building activities by leveraging the existence of the tribe and democratizing the branding process by involving the members of the tribe (Cova and Pace, 2006). As tribes are not as closely linked as communities they tend to be of much greater size and therefore present more economic opportunities for members within. But just like community brands, brands created out of tribes also present value for non-tribe members (von Hippel et al., 2011). Because of their emergence out of their tribe UGBs are deeply embedded in the community of users and live closely with the community. Even though corporate brands also focus on what customers want, provide high quality and innovative products and try to adapt to consumer needs, the connection to their customer base is not shaping their brand in a co-creation sense (Pitt et al., 2006, Füller and Von Hippel, 2008). Virtual worlds enable this close connection of users and product creators and UGBs utilize this setup to shape their brand.

Second, the collective creative process for product development and innovation, which has already been described by Shah and Tripsas (2007) for real life user entrepreneurs and Füller et al. (2007) for community brands, is another defining part in UGBs brand building process. Like-minded individuals often associate with one another and share information, resources and ideas as part of a community (Shah and Tripsas, 2007). This form of information exchange, inherent in virtual worlds, taps enormous creative potential for UGBs and is hard to realize for corporate brands as they are to far away from the community of their users.

The third differentiating characteristic is also a result of the previous two. The closeness of the brands to the users and the collective creative process drive the brand image of authenticity. Users in SL want to be unique, want to express themselves and want to live out their fantasies. UGB as authentic products cater to these wants. Authenticity therefore raises the value of brands to users because, "to serve as valuable ingredients in producing the self, branded cultural resources must be perceived as authentic" (Holt, 2002). SL is a second "reality" for the users and they are therefore not looking for products that resemble the first reality but want to own, do and experience things that only the second "reality" can offer. To be authentic as a brand, this desire of users has to be understood and the products have to resemble the very essence of what the virtual world stands for (e.g. creativity, play, fantasy, etc.) (cp. Chesney et al., 2009). As one participant put it: "*If you're new to SL, spend time in it so you understand the world ... identify a need and meet it*" (Freddy). Being able to provide the uniqueness, genuineness and innovation that users in SL are looking for in a brand gives UGBs the leading edge over real life companies in an environment like SL.

6.5 Conclusions

By examining how UGB use the affordance of virtual worlds to create and build their brands, we showcase the genesis of these brands created within user-generated environments and proposes a set of common characteristics of UGBs.

From a theoretical standpoint, this paper contributes to our understanding of brands in social media environments and adds empirical content to the implied research agenda by Keller's (2009) argument that the reality of brand building in new media environments is more socially constructed today as consumers are taking a more active role in shaping the meaning of brands and is driven by the affordance of these environments. Our research supports two perspectives in information systems and marketing research in connection with virtual worlds: First, this study demonstrates that virtual worlds' affordances offer new options and possibilities for users to act out on their entrepreneurial drive. Second, this study shows that firms derive added value by creatively using willing customer resources (Vargo and Lusch, 2004). Also, by ceding control to customers, brands can enhance consumer engagement and can thereby build brand equity (Pitt et al., 2006, Cova et al., 2007). That said, handing over control for a brand to consumers entails certain risks, such as adaption or hijacking of a brand's meaning (Kates, 2004, Wipperfürth, 2005) and brand resistance and antagonistic behaviour towards brands (Lee, Motion and Conroy 2009; Luedicke, Thompson and Giesler 2010). We argue here that these risks cannot be avoided by trying to protect a brand. Rather UGBs provide inspirations on how to reduce such risks by being more open and engaging.

The results of this study further present insights on the role of authenticity for brands in social media. Our cases show that authenticity, the encapsulation of what consumers perceive as genuine, real and/or true (Beverland et al., 2010, Gilmore and Pine, 2007), cannot simply be transferred from the real world into a virtual world. Adaption of brand and product to the environment based on the understanding of what constitutes the desires of users is necessary to be commercially accepted by the community of users. The advantage of UGBs lies within their naturally evolved understanding of the environment and its users. They leverage existing affordances more effectively and thus better meet the needs of users.

Our analysis of UGBs in SL suggests an increase of "unintentional or accidental entrepreneurship" because of the emerging affordances. Shah and Tripsas (2007) described user entrepreneurship in some niche markets as evolving accidentally, as users develop ideas through own use of a product, share the ideas

6.5 Conclusions

with others and end up commercially exploiting it. Our research showed that creating products and experimenting with ideas is a task users get involved with because of fun and curiosity. Only as those creations turn out to be of value to other users and selling was proposed by co-users, the creators turned their pastime into a commercial activity. Fun and playful activities in virtual worlds like SL could therefore emerge as a driver for entrepreneurship as experimenting with and displaying of creations and inventions becomes easier with the evolution of social media applications (Kozinets et al., 2008).

Furthermore this paper represents the first attempt to describe user-generated brands in a virtual world environment and gives a framework of their characteristics to deepen our understanding on how they emerge and what differentiates them from corporate brands. Even though in the age of social media the differentiation between UGBs and corporate brands might diminish, some fundamental differences will remain. The unintentional nature of this type of entrepreneurship in combination with the unique understanding of the environment will be difficult for corporations to match.

With the description of UGB characteristics, this study also adds to the definition of preconditions for the occurrence of user-entrepreneurship or user-generated brands. Shah and Tripsas (2007) pointed out that conditions likely to favour the emergence of user entrepreneurship include the enjoyment of the original user activity, low opportunity costs, small scale peripheral niche markets with high variety in demand and a relatively turbulent market for the products. The results of our study confirm those favoring conditions for UGBs and add that an environment that fosters rapid or even viral diffusion of information and communication among users and creators is another condition that makes the emergence of UGBs more likely. Through the potential of fast communication flows ideas can find widespread support faster and can reach potential customers easier.

Concerning the attributes of strong brands (Keller, 2000), this study holds some insights on their validity for UGBs and for a potential evolution of those attributes in the future. At large these attributes remain relevant and hold true for UGBs as they concern the provision of excellent and innovative products, understanding the consumer and being present in the mind of consumers and therefore concern core principles of branding that stay valid. Only the way those attributes are achieved or implemented varies with the new and more pro-active role of consumers, which is, to a great extent, attributable to the affordances that virtual worlds and other social media applications offer. However, looking at the communication strategy and the understanding of brand meaning for consumers, two attributes have to be evaluated differently. First, when understanding the role or meaning of brands for consumers, the social value that brands represent to consumers has to be accounted for more strongly – especially as social media influences will positively effect the social nature of brands. Therefore the strength of brands as providers of social value has to be included as one of the attributes of strong brands. Second, conventional communication strategies have to be reconsidered in the light of developments in the communication environment. Communicating consistent messages, associations and images across all elements supporting a brand will be difficult if not impossible considering the evolving pro-active role of consumers in creating meaning for a brand. Therefore, communication strategies for strong brands will have to adapt. UGBs already demonstrate the necessary attributes that are in line with the affordances of a user-generated environment..

From a managerial perspective, this research gives practitioners insights on important brand management aspects in user-generated environments such as virtual worlds. Corporate brands are currently confronted with the challenge of how to effectively leverage the emerging affordances in a co-creation process of brand meaning. This is critical for managers because of four main reasons: First, communication patterns in interactive environments differ significantly from classic brand communication. Secondly, social media environments illustrate specific dynamics of interaction, which influence the perception of branding efforts by relevant customers. Thirdly, many attempts by corporate brands to set foot into social media environments have failed and have left them with a negative image among certain groups of customers. Finally, to maintain strong brands in the future, companies will have to master branding in user-generated environments as strong growth is the shared projection for this trend. UGBs are successful examples of brands built and managed in a virtual world environment. They hold important lessons for corporate brands, which we distilled into a set of recommendations:

Interact playfully with customers to get inspired. Getting and keeping in touch provided the studied UGB with valuable insights for product development. Social media environments like virtual worlds make these interactions easy and abundant, but truly engaging customers asks for entertaining, playful and creative approaches. While the process of constantly interacting with customers is time consuming, brands born in virtual worlds have an edge over corporate brands, because they are enjoying this social process. The playful and entertaining interactions nurture a brands creativity and fuel brand value.

Become one of them: Second Life presents a unique marketplace with its own rules of engagement. To create successful products in this marketplace means to not only understand the users but to become a user. This requires openness and a willingness to invest time to learn about the particular culture of the user-generated environment. The benefit will be deep customer understanding with opportunities to cater to to their needs.

Build the network to foster *word of mouth:* Given the speed of information flow in user-generated environements the relevance of WOM has reached a new level. To foster word-of-mouth in social media, UGB animate influential users to actively create additional related content that is spread among potential customers. The authenticity helps them to build a network of influential followers. Authenticity needs to be maintained regardless of the size of the brand venture, The value of brands for consumers partially comes with its ability to serve as ingredients to produce the self. UGB are perceived to be invented and disseminated without an economic agenda, but rather by intrinsically motivated and likeminded users. By humanizing a brand, companies can learn from UGBs and become more authentic.

Orchestrate a collective creative effort: The participatory environment of virtual worlds implies that people want to be involved in what their favorite brand is doing. Therefore it is important to provide them with the information they are looking for via the channels your customers are using. The most prominent UGB of virtual worlds created a space, where people can meet and interact. Being exposed to the brand supports the creation of brand value – for the company as well as for customers.

This study's limitations, point to promise future research opportunities. First, because of the unique nature of Second Life the transferability to other social media environments needs to be treated with caution. Further research in other social media environments is necessary to strengthen our understanding of brands in user-generated environments and whether the lessons learned also hold true in other social media environments. Second, we have focused on the perspective of the brand creator to show how creators of brands in SL go about managing their brands and thereby we emphasized the management side of the process of the creation of brand meaning. As the process of creating brand meaning involves all stakeholders and different kinds of brand manifestations (Mühlbacher and Hemetsberger, 2008, Merz et al., 2009) this research can only cover a small part in the perspective of brand meaning creation in SL. To get a more complete picture on how brand meaning is created, the co-creation process of brand meaning has to be studied using various perspectives and a more holistic approach (cp. Diamond et al., 2009). Thirdly, this paper focuses on UGBs in the virtual world SL. As other virtual worlds are constantly created and high growth for virtual goods is projected, the appearance of UGBs in other virtual worlds should be another avenue for future research. Also, future research might look for similar brand building efforts in other social media applications and describe the prerequisites of those applications that favor the creation of UGBs. Finally, we were able to show and describe the existence of UGBs on a case study basis, but to further prove the widespread success of those brands in SL, economic data from Linden Lab or other quantitative data on those grass-roots brands in SL and other social media applications would be necessary.

Whether or not the future of the internet will be virtual worlds (Hopkins, 2009, de Mesa, 2007, de Mesa, 2009), we are convinced that UGBs provide both a promising new research area and a source for inspiration for managing brands within social media environments.

6.6 Appendix – Interviewguideline

Beginning in SL

- *Can you share your story of how you started to create your own products in SL?*
- *How did you first come up with the idea of building your own business?*
    - Why did you get started in SL?
    - Was it a group effort or a single initiative? If group effort, how did the collaboration work (who did what, what were the difficulties, …)?
    - Was it a planned effort from the start or did it just happen?
    - Would you describe your business as commercial or non-commercial?

General Understanding of Brands

- *What do you think are customers looking for in a product/brand?*
    - What do you think makes customers buy certain products or shop in certain locations?
- *From your point of view, what makes your strongest competitors distinctive as businesses/brands and who are they?*
    - For you, what are the most important characteristics of a brand?

- *What makes your own business/brand distinctive?*
  - Would you describe your business as a brand? Why/why not?
  - How would you describe your brand?
  - When would you say that a brand is successful?
  - What does success in SL mean to you?
  - How important is it to have a brand name in SL and why?

Brand Management and Marketing Mix

- *If you would start a brand new business in SL, could you describe how you would build your business/brand?*
- *What are the most important aspects of promoting your brand?*
  - Advertisement, means of communication, price, ...
- *What role do the users/community around your business play for the success of your business?*
  - How important is it to create a community around a business/brand?
  - How did you build a community?
  - How do you try to manage/influence the community?
  - How did you rely on the community? How did they support you?
  - How did the community react when the business turned commercial?
- *For you, how would the ideal distribution strategy for your products in SL look like?*
- *What are critical threats for your brand and how do you deal with them?*
- *From your point of view, what are the critical success factors for establishing a successful brand in SL?*

Closing Questions

- *Have you thought about expanding into "real life" with your brand?*
- *Why do you think real life brands failed in SL?*
- *What makes the value of a successful brand?*
- *Do you have any other comments?*

Additional Questions

- When did you start your business in Second Life?
- Can you live of your Second Life profits?
- How much money did you invest at the beginning?
- How many hours per week do you usually invest in your SL business?
- How much revenue did you generate in 2009? What is your average revenue per month? Are you among the top 1% of merchants in SL?
- How many customers did you serve in the last month?
- How many employees do you have?

Demographic Questions

- How long have you been in Second Life?
- What is your real life age?
- Are you the same gender as your avatar?

7 Perception of User-generated Brands: A New Power in the Minds of Consumers?

7.1 Introduction

The emergence and rise of social media and web 2.0 technologies have made user-generated content one of the driving forces of online experiences. User-generated content (UGC), for example in the form of user reviews or blog posts, is one of the most influential sources of online information today. But users have also started to distribute and sell their own UGC and have thereby accomplished the creation of brands: so-called user-generated brands (UGB). Apache and Linux are among the most famous examples of brands created by users (Pitt, Watson, Berthon, Wynn, & Zinkhan, 2006; Schroll, Hemetsberger, & Füller, 2010). Similar brands were also found to be formed in online communities (Füller, Lüdicke, & Jawecki, 2007) and by individuals in virtual worlds (Dennhardt, Kohler, & Füller, 2011).

Recently the notion that users can establish businesses and brands is gaining traction. This trend is supported by findings on innovation activities by users (Lüthje, Herstatt, & von Hippel, 2005; E. von Hippel, 1988; Eric von Hippel, 2005) and research that has identified innovative users to become "accidental" entrepreneurs (Shah & Tripsas, 2007). In brand research the notion of the influential and active user has also been recognized (Cova, Dalli, & Zwick, 2011; Kozinets, de Valck, Wojnicki, & Wilner, 2010; Merz, Yi, & Vargo, 2009). To date, literature on brands that are created by users rather than simply influenced, modified or captured by them is rare. Pitt et al. (2006) point out that the Open Source movement has produced some well-know brands like Apache and Linux, which were effectively created and established by users and which exhibit features "like any other brand". Research on the Apache brand (Eric von Hippel, Schroll, & Füller, 2011) shows that users can not only generate valuable brands for the user community, where it was initiated, but that those brands can also create strong associations outside of the user-community.

Although it has been shown that user-generated brands exhibit value, commercialization has mostly not occurred. It is therefore difficult to demonstrate the immediate value of UGBs. Nevertheless, as UGBs have been recognized and accepted by consumers, they must exhibit value for them. Pitt et al. (2006) and von Hippel et al. (2011) argue that user-generated brands possess value to consumers beyond what corporate brands can offer, since brands created by users offer different utilities. This research sets out to empirically test what kind of utility user-generated brands exhibit to consumers and how this utility is valued by consumers and differentiates itself in comparison to corporate brands. This study therefore investigates the psychological, sociological and practical benefits of those brands for consumers as potential drivers of competitive advantage.

With an experimental setup in the context of freeskiing brands, we test if consumers perceive a difference between commercial brands and brands created by users in respect to the dimensions of sympathy, authenticity and credibility, which are considered as strong drivers of value from a consumer perspective. Our findings of the experiment with 804 users show that brands which are generated by users and communities indeed are perceived as more sympathetic and authentic. From a theoretical standpoint the results are relevant as they firstly add to our understanding of the occurrence of brands created by users. Secondly, they help us to better understand the utility of those brands from a consumer perspective. For brand managers the results are of interest as they shed light on a potentially challenging phenomenon for contemporary brand management and reveal potential shortcomings of corporate brands from the point of consumers.

7.2 Conceptual Foundations

7.2.1 The Value of Brands for Consumers

For consumers the value of brands is based on the functions and utilities they provide (Keller, 2008; Riesenbeck & Perrey, 2007). In other words, a brand's perceived value for a consumer is the total sum of the physical and psychological benefits the consumer receives from the brand (Avery, et al., 2010). According to brand literature (cp. Kapferer, 2008; Muniz & O'Guinn, 2001), the perceived value stems from four distinct benefit dimensions: informational, risk reducing, symbolic and identity related and social. First, brands are carriers of information (cp. Kapferer, 2008; Keller, 2008). They let consumers easily recognise and identify products and give them information about the origin and quality of the product. They thereby lower search costs as they allow time and energy saving through repurchasing and loyalty. Secondly, brands lower consumers' perceived risk of making a wrong purchase decision. They indicate a certain level of quality, ensure the expected performance and attest social acceptance. To serve these two rather mechanical functions, brands need to be perceived by consumers as trustworthy and as having expertise. Third, brands support consumers in their creation of a self-concept and a social identity and therefore exhibit a symbolic function (Ahuvia, 2005; Belk, 1988; Escalas & Bettman, 2005; Fournier, 1998). For consumers, brands are a repository of meanings (Fournier, 1998) and, hence, serve as powerful symbolic and cultural resources for individual identity projects (Holt, 2002; McCracken, 1989). Consumers tend to prefer brand meaning that matches with their self-image as they are better suited for their identity projects (Aaker, Fournier, & Brasel, 2004). To serve as valuable ingredients of meaning for the creation of identity, brands must be perceived as authentic and sympathetic by consumers and must be offered as cultural resources (Holt, 2002). Fourth, and yet not widely acknowledged, brands exhibit a social function as they support the building of relationships and social ties and foster social integration (Cova, 1997; Muniz & O'Guinn, 2001; Schau, Muniz, & Arnould, 2009). Cova (1997) for example argues that consumers value products and services less for their use value and more for their linking value – for their ability to enable and facilitate bonds between individuals.

7.2.2 Utility of User Generated Brands

For UGBs to be valuable to consumers, they need to not only present utility to consumers, but they need to distinguish themselves from larger commercial brands in order to be recognized by the market. Based on branding theory, we suggest that UGBs can distinguish themselves from competing commercial brands along four dimensions: price, authenticity, knowledge, and rejection of commercial brands. First, as Pitt et al. (2006) have pointed out, UGBs can offer a potential financial benefit for consumers by either being distributed for free or by reducing brand premiums from commercial brands. Second, following Holt (2002), a brand needs to be perceived as authentic as this is the prerequisite for a brand to be considered an ingredient in constructing the self. To be experienced as authentic, "brands must be disinterested; they must be perceived as invented and disseminated by parties without an instrumental agenda, by people who are intrinsically motivated by their inherent value" (Holt, 2002, p. 83). Brands created by users, in contrast to corporate brands, exhibit those essential characteristics giving them an authentic image. Third, users that are starting a business apply their own use-experience and know-how to cater more precisely to the needs of consumers (Baldwin, Hienerth, & von Hippel, 2006). They establish themselves in niche markets and offer products that have a unique and often new use-value (Franke & Shah, 2003). The users creating UGBs are usually experts in the field of the product, mostly through extensive use-experience, which provides them with the necessary knowledge to develop new products that are superior to existing ones. Various examples in the sports industry have shown that (Franke & Shah, 2003). Together, this gives UGBs a certain degree of credibility, even if they have not been in business for long. User-generated brands are more tailored to the needs of consumers (from users for users) and can therefore better serve consumers' identity projects as they are more sympathetic to consumers and their claims are perceived more credible. Fourth, as a considerable part of consumers tends to dislike big commercial brands (Holt, 2002), UGBs offer a viable and more sympathetic alternative to escape the mass market. In Germany for example, a group of users has established a small soft drink company called "Premium Cola", once the producer abandoned the old recipe of their favourite Afri Cola, as a kind of counter reaction to the likes of Coca-Cola.

Overall, we argue that user-generated brands, compared to commercial brands, may provide certain advantages from the viewpoint of consumers. Therefore, this study proposes that the origin of a brand does influence the perception of the brand in respect to sympathy, authenticity and credibility. These relationships are summarized in Hypothesis H1a to H1c.

> H1a: A brand created by users is perceived as more sympathetic than a brand created by a large commercial brand.
>
> H1b: A brand created by users is perceived as more authentic than a brand created by a large commercial brand.
>
> H1c: A brand created by users is perceived as more credible than a brand created by a large commercial brand.

The proposed relationships between the origin of the brand and the perception of the brand should be valid for consumers overall, even if they are not using the product themselves or are not highly involved with the product. For extensive users of the product, who are themselves very knowledgeable in the product category and are highly involved with the product, the relationships should be even stronger. The rationale for this is the stronger identification with the origin of the brand. Since involved users regularly use the product and usually deal with other users, they can relate and identify with other extensive users (McAlexander, Schouten, & Koenig, 2002; Muniz & O'Guinn, 2001). In the case of a

UGB, other users will feel a connection to the founder(s) of the brand and hence the brand itself, which they wouldn't feel with an anonymous firm. Hypotheses H2a to H2c summarize the relationships.

> H2a: For extensive users of the product category, a brand created by users within this category is perceived as more sympathetic than a brand created by a large commercial firm.
>
> H2b: For extensive users of the product category, a brand created by users within this category is perceived as more authentic than a brand created by a large commercial firm.
>
> H2c: For extensive users of the product category, a brand created by users within this category is perceived as more credible than a brand created by a large commercial firm.

7.3 Method and Study Design

To test for the effects of different origins of a brand an experimental design was used. A one-factor between subjects design was devised in an online setting with three experimental groups and one control group. Participants were tested after exposure to the stimulus. Freeskiing equipment was selected as the investigated product category. Freeskiing can be described as a subculture of skiing, in many ways similar to snowboarding. A total of 804 respondents voluntarily participated in the experiment based on invocations via a mailing list at a European university, via a freeskiing online-platform (downdays.eu) and via social networks. Participants were asked to take part in a survey on the perception of brands. Respondents followed a link to an online questionnaire that randomly assigned them to one of the four treatment groups. They were presented with one out of four short articles about a fictitious freeskiing brand (see Figure 4). The articles were identical except for the originator of the brand, who was named at three different places in the text. Depending on the experimental group the participants were assigned to, the originator in the article was either a passionate user (group 1), i.e. a freeskier himself, a community of freeskiers (group 2), or a large sports company (group 3). We used two forms of UGBs, i.e., user and community brand, in order to control for a potentially higher perceived expertise with multiple users in a community. The article of the control group (group 4) con-

> **Hiatus - A newborn Star**
>
> Hiatus is a newborn star among brands in the freeskiing-scene. The brand was founded by Mitch Zapik, himself a passionate freeskier. He came up with the brand name and the logo and is creating the designs for its freeskiing equipment like skis, poles, beanies, t-shirts or gloves himself – all specifically aimed at freeski enthusiasts. The products are produced by one of the main suppliers for skiing-equipment. The founder wants Hiatus to stand for the real spirit of freeskiing, which essentially is a free-minded movement within skiing centred around powder and freestyle. It thereby aims at delivering to the desire to combine style and performance.

Figure 4: Article as presented in the experiment (user brand)

tained no reference to an originator. After they read the article, participants were asked to fill out a survey.

In the survey following the experimental stimulus the dependent variables sympathy, authenticity and credibility were measured: sympathy was measured using three items from Fischer et al. (2010) ($\alpha = 0,92$); to measure authenticity, this study used five items based on Wood et al. (Wood, Linley, Maltby, Baliousis, & Joseph, 2008) ($\alpha = 0,88$); and the credibility measure consisted of five items based on Erdem and Swait (1998) and Ohanian (1990) ($\alpha = 0,88$). All items were measured using a seven-point semantic differential scale with the anchors "strongly agree" (1) and "strongly disagree" (7). The measured control variables included measurements for expected quality (three items based on Erdem and Swait (1998) and Pappu et al. (2005)), for perceived risks (two items based on Erdem and Swait (2004)), for brand relevance (four items based on Fischer et al. (2010)), for product involvement (three items based on Beatty and Talpade (1994)), for need for uniqueness (four items based on Tian et al. (2001)) and for attitude towards corporations (one item based on Richins (1983)). To make sure participants were able to distinguish between the different brand-sources, we indirectly checked for manipulation by asking for the effect that a purchase of the presented brand by a commercial brand would have on the perception of sympathy and authenticity. For the manipulation to be successful, the difference between UGBs and the corporate brand would have to be significant.

7.4 Results

A series of analyses of variance (ANOVAs), including post-hoc tests (least significant differences), were conducted to analyse whether the four groups differ with regard to the control variables. The analyses revealed no significant differences for all control variables. This is important as it shows that the manipulation

7.4 Results

was insofar successful as differences in the dependent variables could not be attributable to differences in the control variables.

The treatment showed to be effective as participants evaluated the effect of a corporate acquisition significantly less negative for groups 1 (M_{sym} = 3,56; M_{auth} = 3,12) and 2 (M_{sym} = 3,86; M_{auth} = 3,13) than for groups 3 (M_{sym} = 4,04; M_{auth} = 3,51) and 4 (M_{sym} = 4,22; M_{auth} = 3,52) (F_{sym} = 5,56; $p < 0,001$; F_{auth} = 3,61; $p < 0,02$; post hoc test $p < 0,05$). This demonstrates that a difference in the origins of the brands was perceived, and hence the manipulation was effective.

Results from ANOVAs show that the origin of brand has a significant effect on sympathy, supporting hypothesis H1a, and on authenticity, supporting hypothesis H1b (see Table 4). Since results showed no significant differences for the perception of credibility, H1c was not supported. Confirming these results, we tested for differences between the two user-generated brand origins (user brand and community brand, N = 391) and the corporate origin. Results showed that significant differences were perceived for sympathy (T = 1,98 , $p < 0,05$) and authenticity (T = 4,71 , $p < 0,001$). This means that the origins of a brand do have a strong influence on how sympathetic and how authentic a consumer perceives a brand. Brands with a user origin score better for authenticity and sympathy in comparison to the corporate origin.

Taking the target group for the presented brand, i.e. the freeskiers, results were stronger as hypothesis H2a and H2b were supported and hypothesis H2c was somewhat supported (see Table 1). This shows that with involved users, that are closer to other peers, the perception in respect to sympathy and authenticity also varies significantly between the groups. With the group of freeskiers, results for the user-generated origin group (N = 76) and the corporate origin group (N = 58) show significant differences for sympathy (T = 2,52 , $p < ,05$), authenticity (2,94 , $p < ,01$), and credibility (T = 2,13 , $p < ,05$), which supports hypotheses H2a to H2c.

Further conducted MANOVAs with gender, age (two groups: <31 and >31) and user-expertise (freeskier and non freeskier) as additional independent variables showed no significant interaction effects for gender and user-expertise, but significant effects for age regarding the dependent variables authenticity and credibility ($p < 0.05$). This shows that the origin of the brand has a different effect on the two age groups in respect to their perception of authenticity and credibility.

Table 4: Findings (post hoc tests: p < 0,05)

Dependent Variables		User Brand (N = 200) M (SD)	Community Brand (N = 191) M (SD)	Corporate Brand (N = 197) M (SD)	Control Group (N = 216) M (SD)	F-Value (p-Value)
Sympathy	Overall (N = 804)	3,13 (1,1)	2,97 (1,08)	3,26 (1,26)	3,03 (1,15)	2,36 (0,07)
	Freeskier (N = 199)	2,78 (0,88)	2,82 (0,89)	3,34 (1,46)	2,73 (0,98)	3,73 (0,01)
Authenticity	Overall (N = 804)	2,97 (1,14)	2,92 (1,02)	3,44 (1,26)	3,13 (1,18)	8,07 (<0,001)
	Freeskier (N = 199)	2,91 (1,03)	2,99 (0,98)	3,57 (1,35)	3,14 (1,27)	3,01 (0,03)
Credibility	Overall (N = 804)	3,33 (1,14)	3,44 (1,08)	3,48 (1,16)	3,46 (1,2)	0,63 (>0,1)
	Freeskier (N = 199)	3,07 (0,92)	3,22 (1,05)	3,57 (1,29)	3,23 (1,13)	1,83 (0,14)

7.5 Discussion, Implications and Limitations

The results from this study show that consumers perceive brands that were created by users, i.e. by a single user or a community of users, differently than a brand created by a firm. A significant difference in the perception of the brand's sympathy and authenticity could be demonstrated. These results point to a value-adding utility of user-created brands, which distinguishes them from commercial brands and could be an advantage in competition.

The most significant effect was found for authenticity. Defined as the encapsulation of what is genuine, real and/or true (Arnould & Price, 2000; Beverland, Farrelly, & Quester, 2010), authenticity, from a consumer perspective, derives its importance today from the shift towards a more experience-driven economy (Gilmore & Pine, 2007). In combination with an increase in technology-driven interactions, a postmodernistic and socially constructed reality and a loss of trust in established institutions, an increasingly unreal world, filled with deliberately and sensationally staged experiences, drives consumers to buy what they perceive as real, original, sincere, and genuine – in short, authentic (Gilmore & Pine, 2007; Henderson & Bowley, 2010). Similarly, the loss of traditional sources of meaning and self-identity caused by postmodernism (Arnould & Price, 2000) and the standardization and homogenization in the marketplace (Thompson, Rindfleisch, & Arsel, 2006) have been identified as drivers for the active and adept appropriation of authenticity in consumption patterns.

Sympathy, which was also shown to be higher for brands created by users, supports the symbolic utility of a brand (Ahuvia, 2005; Carroll & Ahuvia, 2006). To function as an ingredient for the creation of the self, the perception of a brand as sympathetic is important. As consumers look for a congruency between the characteristics of a brand and their own (perceived) characteristics, sympathy is a prerequisite for brands to be considered as an ingredient in identity projects, because without sympathy congruence is not possible. When user-generated brands are perceived as more sympathetic, may it be because they are perceived as the "underdog" or may it be because consumers find it easier to identify with a brand that is perceived to be more closely related to the use-experience, utility and thus value is added for consumers.

Concerning credibility, no significant differences were found in the overall sample. Credibility composes itself from trustworthiness and expertise (Erdem & Swait, 1998). Considering an established brand, it can be expected that consumers evaluate the trustworthiness of the brand higher, as it possesses legitimacy through longer existence. UGBs, in contrast, do not possess a long history of successful catering to consumers' needs, and hence, their trustworthiness can be expected to be evaluated lower. Established brands also stand for technical expertise. However, UGBs' expertise through use-experience might be valued higher by other users. Hence, these two effects could balance each other out. Therefore, a significant difference could only be shown for the sample of the extensive users, who valued the local knowledge and expertise of users strongest. Furthermore, the interaction effect for the two age groups indicates that younger consumers tend to perceive credibility differently than older consumers when it comes to brand origins. A possible reason is that younger consumers put more emphasis on innovativeness and performance, whereas older consumers focus more on dependability.

From a theoretical standpoint, this study contributes to our understanding of the emerging phenomenon of brands created by users. It supports the notion that those brands exhibit additional value for consumers, but goes beyond the findings of Pitt et al. (2006) as it shows sources of this additional value, besides the financial ones. Furthermore this study explains why consumers favour user-generated brands compared to commercial brands and thereby also demonstrates a competitive advantage that those brands might have.

From a managerial perspective the results of this study are relevant as they give insights on a potentially challenging phenomenon for established brands. Various studies have shown the relevance of authenticity for consumer self-conception in consumption (Holt, 2002; Kates, 2004; Thompson, et al., 2006). This could indicate the possibility that user-created brands could conquer a market niche where consumers have a high relevance for the authenticity of brands. This study thereby also demonstrates potential shortcomings of commercial brands and shows potential areas of improvement with respect to their branding efforts.

This study also has limitations that lead to future research possibilities: Our research was the first one to consider the effect of brand origins on consumers' perception of sympathy, authenticity and credibility. Future research could use different dependent variables and include financial measures like willingness-to-pay. Also, a brand from a different high-involvement product category could be tested to further validate the results.

8 The Value-enhancing Role of Social Networks Around Brands: The Concept of Social Brand Value

8.1 Introduction

Firms are facing a new marketing communication reality that has been created by the rise of social media. The widespread penetration of web 2.0 applications, in combination with faster and greater mobile computing power and advances in bandwidth, has enabled this revolution. Applications like Facebook and YouTube have created a revolutionary trend, influencing communication habits (Henderson and Bowley 2010). As consumers are becoming more familiar with advanced communication and media technologies, they now have to be recognized as active creators, instead of passive, consuming participants (Henderson and Bowley 2010; Kozinets et al. 2008; Merz et al. 2009; Qualman 2011; Vargo and Lusch 2004). Users adopt and customize online tools available to them to transform digital space into a profoundly social eco-system they can create, control and own (Mooney and Rollins 2008).

The interactive nature of the Internet has empowered individuals to directly engage with brands and other users, and has upset the power balance between the firm and the individual by shifting more of the control over brands from producers directly to consumers (Constantinides and Fountain 2008). The handling of marketing in the challenging social media environment is therefore one of the most relevant topics for executives today (Barwise and Meehan 2010).

Companies accept the relevance of social media for consumers and, thus, try to create and maintain a presence in social networks – the place where the consumer is (Barwise and Meehan 2010; Day 2011; Hoffman and Fodor 2010). To this end, they create fan pages on Facebook, establish Twitter accounts, support blogs or enter into virtual worlds in order to enchant their "fans" and foster the creation of user-generated content and word-of-mouth. Experience has shown that not all brands are equally able to attract online communities and spur interactions among consumers. Some brands do not seem sufficiently attractive to consumers in respect to their social and entertainment potential, while Apple, Starbucks and Google are examples of companies that have been able to manage their social media engagements with consumers successfully (cp. Engagementdb 2009).

To this point, it is unclear how important the ability of brands to foster social interactions is to consumers and how this might influence the valuation of brands. So far, research on concepts for measuring brand value from a consumer's perspective – mainly the brand equity concept (Keller 1993) – has not included a social, relationship-based perspective. Given the importance and relevance of social ties, social interactions and social identity in the new media environment, there is a growing need to account for a relationship measure in contemporary marketing and branding. This study therefore investigates how the social attractiveness of a brand for consumers influences their valuation of the brand and if practice should account for a social measure when evaluating brands.

From a theoretical standpoint, the results of this study are relevant, as they firstly contribute to our understanding of the value-enhancing potential of social capital and its dimensions on economic capital (i.e., brand equity) of brands and secondly add to our overall understanding of the social role that brands exhibit. For brand managers, our findings are relevant, as they demonstrate sustainable effects of social media presences and the potential value enhancements of these social-media activities to brands.

Based on the concept of social capital (Bourdieu 1984), we introduce the concept of social brand value, defined as the perceived value consumers derive from the exchange and interactions with other users centered around the brand. The social brand value is embedded in the social network and social ties offered by the brand. In contrast to this consumer perspective, social brand value from companies' perspective is the part of the overall brand value that arises from social networks and interactions of brand users. In this paper, we focus on the consumer perspective and show that the social brand value influences consumers' willingness to pay a price premium (WTP) and engage in brand evangelism.

After giving an overview on the brand equity concept, social capital theory, and brand value creation from interactions in the following section of the paper, we introduce the social brand value construct and describe its potential value driving effects. The empirical study – a survey conducted with 1,301 participants on 19 brands – demonstrates the influence the social brand value construct has for consumers' brand evangelism and willingness to pay a price premium and, hence, the value contribution of the social brand value for consumers.

8.2 Theoretical Background

8.2.1 The Brand Equity Concept

The functions of a brand are the source of its value and hence its equity. The utilities or functions of a brand can be analyzed from the perspectives of brand owners and consumers. Whereas brand owners build and sustain brands mainly for profit-seeking purposes, the utility of brands for consumers has three distinct dimensions. First, the more functional benefits for consumers encompass the informational and risk-reducing role of brands (cp. Kapferer 2008; Keller 2008). Second, brands support consumers in their creation of self-concept and social identity and therefore exhibit a symbolic function (Ahuvia 2005; Belk 1988; Escalas and Bettman 2005; Fournier 1998). For consumers, brands are a powerful source of meaning (Fournier 1998) and, hence, serve as powerful symbolic resources for individual identity projects (McCracken 1989). Third, and yet not widely acknowledged, brands exhibit a social function as they support the building of relationships and social ties and foster social integration (Cova 1997; Muniz and O'Guinn 2001; Schau et al. 2009). The idea of brand equity is based on these benefits.

The concept of brand equity has attracted a lot of attention since it first emerged in the late 1980s. As companies started to see their brands as valuable assets, and as brand management moved from a supportive function to the core of many businesses, the interest in conceptualizing, measuring and managing the value of the brand (i.e., brand equity) increased (Keller 1993). Since then, many scholars have contributed to the advancement of our understanding of brand equity and ways to measure it (Aaker 1991; Aaker 1996; Farquhar 1990; Kapferer 2008; Keller 1993; Pappu et al. 2005). Although a vast number of definitions of brand equity exist, most of them are based on Farquhar's definition (Aaker 1991; Farquhar 1990; Keller 1993; Srivastava and Shocker 1991). He defined brand equity "as the added value with which a given brand endows a product" (Farquhar 1990, p. 7).

Nevertheless, different viewpoints exist on what brand equity consists of: loyalty and image (Shocker and Weitz 1988); brand loyalty, brand awareness, perceived quality, brand associations, and other proprietary brand assets (Aaker 1991); the added value endowed by the brand name (Farquhar 1990); incremental utility (Kamakura and Russell 1993); brand knowledge such as brand awareness and brand associations (Keller 1993); favorable impressions, attitudinal dispositions, and behavioral predilections (Rangaswamy et al. 1993); the difference between overall brand preference and multi-attributed preference based on objectively measured attribute levels (Park and Srinivasan 1994); or, overall quality and choice intention (Agarwal and Rao 1996).

Some of the core elements of brand equity are brand loyalty or brand evangelism, perceived quality and, as a direct measure of the added value of a brand, willingness to pay a price premium. Brand evangelism (BE) is the willingness of consumers to act as ambassadors of the brand and to convince other consumers to buy it (Carroll and Ahuvia 2006; Schau et al. 2009). BE thereby goes beyond brand loyalty, which reduces the risk of consumers switching to another brand (Aaker 1991), as it stands for consumers' willingness to proactively show and convince others of their object of loyalty. Especially in light of the rise of social media, the hype around "I like" recommendations and the ease of peer-to-peer communication, direct referencing and recommending has increased in importance for consumer decision-making (Zhu and Zhang 2010). Perceived quality (PQ) refers to consumer's subjective judgment of the quality of a product or service (Zeithaml et al. 1988) and provides value to the consumer by reducing perceived risks and differentiating the brand from competing brands (Pappu et al. 2005). WTP is the willingness to pay an excess price for a brand, over and above the "fair" price that is justified by the "true" value of the product (Rao and Bergen 1992). It is thereby a direct measure of the additional financial value that a brand is able to generate. Taken together, these elements represent some core features of the brand-equity idea.

As brands developed from being simple markers of identification to complex social phenomena, which play a central role in consumer society, our perspective on the value a brand provides has to be adapted. Although the consumer-based brand equity perspective is broadly accepted today (Keller 1993), it still puts too much emphasis on brand managers' actions. It thereby neglects consumers' active role in the value-creation process (Bengtsson and Ostberg 2004) and ignores developments in the marketing-communication environment (Keller 2009). "The more socially constructed brand building reality" (Keller 2009, p. 153) today asks for a rethinking of branding concepts like brand knowledge, meaning and equity. Muniz and O'Guinn (2001) have shown that brand community indirectly affects brand equity by influencing its components (e.g. brand loyalty, perceived quality). However, as consumers get some value-in-use from participating in communities and building brand-related relationships with other consumers (Merz et al. 2009; Schau et al. 2009), the social nature of a brand is to be understood as a direct value-determining component of brand equity.

Despite the many different approaches of how to compose brand equity and the acknowledgement of the social nature of brands, literature has not yet considered the inclusion of the social component of brands as part of the brand-equity concept. As Bourdieu (1986) described resources based on social networks as a form of capital, we argue that the social value of a brand is an important part of its equity. The value of social ties has therefore to be accounted for when measuring a brand's value and evaluating the success of marketing campaigns (with particular respect to social media marketing).

8.2.2 Social Capital and the Creation of Value through Relationships and Interactions

Bourdieu (1984) described the social world as a multidimensional space in which differentiation happens through different types of resources or capital from which people draw. It follows that this social space is structured according to the distribution of various forms of capital, which have the capability to confer strength and power and consequently profit their holder. Bourdieu (1986) essentially differentiates among three types of capital: economic, cultural and social capital. Economic capital comprises everything that is "immediately and directly convertible into money" (Bourdieu 1986, p. 243) and is institutionalized in the form of property rights. Cultural capital consists of "socially rare and distinctive tastes, skills, knowledge, and practices" (Holt 1998, p. 3) and appears in three primary forms embodied as "implicit practical knowledge, skills, and disposetions; objectified in cultural objects; and institutionalized in official degrees and diplomas" (Holt 1998, p. 3). Social capital is defined as the entirety of actual and potential resources that arise from more or less durable networks of institutionalized relationships (Bourdieu 1986). In other words, social capital gives its holder access to resources embedded in social networks that he may use and from which he may profit (Esser 2008; Lin 2001). Economic capital can be used to build the latter two forms of capital through efforts of transformation. Conversely, cultural and social capital exhibit value for the holder as they convey status and can be converted, under certain conditions, into economic capital (Bourdieu 1986). In respect to social capital, an individual holder can use his social relations to borrow or capture other actors' resources in order to generate profit for himself (Lin 2001). For example, a social actor might get valuable information concerning a lucrative investment opportunity, or he might be able to get a better medical treatment through his relations to influential doctors. The ability to convert social capital thereby depends on the structural position of the actor in the network, the strength of the ties within the network, the purpose of access (i.e., instrumental or for maintaining cohesion, solidarity, or well-being) and the skills in conducting the conversion (Lin 2001).

In contrast to the other forms of capital, social capital is purely relational, as it entails resources based on membership to social groups (Vogt 2000). The profits, which accrue through this membership, are the basis for solidarity, which in turn makes the profits possible (Bourdieu 1986). These profits or returns arise from three typical forms of social resources and benefits provided by relations and networks: social integration, symbolic or identity value and access to knowledge. First, through membership to a group or community, individuals in the network experience mutual trust, solidarity and support (Esser 2008) and receive social credentials (Lin 2001). Second, as relations based on interactions form social capital, and as identity is a product of interactions and highly dependable on the social space in which these interactions take place, social capital plays a central role in the building of people's identity and therefore exhibits identity value to the holder (Lin 2001; Vogt 2000). Third, social capital presents value to its holder as it grants access to knowledge and information within social networks (Esser 2008; Lin 2001).

Relationships and ties formed in an online environment create (social) value as they represent social capital. Value-creating relationships that constitute social capital are independent of the proximity of these relations in geographical, economic or social space (Bourdieu 1986). Therefore, it doesn't matter if the relevant network ties are situated in an offline or online context. As relationships today are significantly influenced by developments of detraditionalization and individualization (Vogt 2000), and as social interactions are happening more and more in online environments, social online networks play an increasingly important role in the creation of people's social capital.

8.2.3 Social Capital of Brands

The connection between social capital theory and branding theory is grounded within the social nature of brands and its encompassing benefits for customers. Because of the social function of brands, consumption and preference of a brand can help in building relationships and forming a sense of community (McAlexander et al. 2002, Muniz and O'Guinn 2001). Research into brand communities demonstrated that a shared consciousness, rituals and traditions, and a sense of moral responsibility form and hold together affectionate communities around brands (Muniz and Schau 2005) and thereby build the foundation for the social nature of brands (Muniz and O'Guinn 2001). McAlexander et al. (2003) proposed that it is through consumer experience that the existence and benefits of the relationships of a brand community unfold. These relationships develop synergistically, strengthening interpersonal ties and enhancing appreciation for the product and the brand, which integrates customers into the brand community and encourages loyalty (McAlexander et al. 2003). Cova (1997) argues, that consumers in the postmodern era value products, services and brands more for their linking value – for their ability to enable and facilitate bonds between individuals – and less for their sheer utility value as they enable and support social interactions and relationships of the communal type. In accordance, Schau et al. (2009) proposed that the emergent sense of community membership and identity creates value for members through "the exchange of collectively defined and valorized resources" (Schau et al. 2009, p. 35).

The brand thus derives value and meaning from community integration, and consumers benefit from the brand, as it offers a linking value by connecting like-minded people and by facilitating cues of tying people together into networks. Social connections, enabled by communities and other brand-related relationships, represent potentially valuable resources for consumers and therefore increase the value of the brand – what we call social brand value (SBV) – for consumers and, hence, for companies. Applying Bourdieu's theory of capital, the value consumers receive from social interactions and relations in connection with a brand can be described as part of consumers' social capital. Brands present to consumers a way to interact and relate to other consumers and thus to build social capital. Hence, one of the main purposes a brand these days is consumed is for its ability to serve as a means for social integration, identity building and information access. Through these profit sources, consumers receive additional returns for the social capital a brand represents.

Putting it differently, the social capital a brand offers stems from being relevant in social networks and, thereby, providing individuals the possibilities to connect and interact with each other about the meaning and experiences that a brand offers. Taking into account current developments with online social networks, fast-paced formation of online communities, and increased relevance of relationships and social ties for brands, this perspective on the value of brands can derive interesting insights on the perception of brand value. Nevertheless, contemporary brand models insufficiently consider the impact of the linking value or social value of a brand on its overall economic value. In the next section, we introduce the social brand value model, which addresses those shortcomings of existing models.

8.3 Conceptual Model

The framework shown in Figure 5 summarizes the hypothesized effects of social brand value on overall brand value, reflected in consumers' willingness to pay a price premium and engage in evangelism for the brand, the perceived quality-brand value relationship, and the perceived quality-SBV relationship.

For our study, the constructs of willingness to pay a price premium and brand evangelism (as two important measures for brand equity) serve to test the value-adding potential of social brand value for consumers. Social brand value, as part of the social capital represented by brands, constitutes a resource for consumers. The holders of this socially constructed resource, which is inherent in social capital, can use it to acquire profits. This transformation thereby works by means of converting social capital into economic capital (Lin 2001). To enable control for a quality effect, the value-enhancing role of perceived quality and its proposed positive effect on brand value is also included in this model.

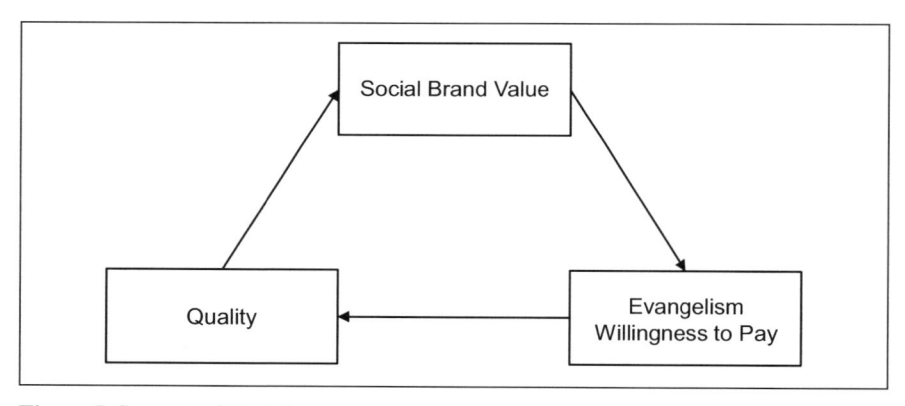

Figure 5: Conceptual Model

8.3.1 Quality and its Impact on Brand Value

Perceived quality is one of the main requirements for brands to generate additional value for consumers. By purchasing brands, consumers want to reduce the risk of not getting the expected quality of a product. A strong connection between perceived quality and the perceived value of a brand (i.e., consumers' willingness to pay a price premium and brand evangelism) is the consequence.

Willingness to pay a price premium represents a financial measure of the value that consumers are willing to invest to buy a brand that has a higher perceived (social) brand value. Brand evangelism, in contrast, represents a less tangible approach to value. It refers to the active recommending of brands to other consumers and the advocating of brands (cp. Carroll and Ahuvia 2006). The value exhibiting function of brand evangelism is based on the recommending and advocating behavior of consumers and is thereby better suited to show the social value of a brand than, for example, brand loyalty or brand love. Brand loyalty, in essence, only reflects repeat-purchase behavior or the respective intentions (McAlexander et al. 2003) but doesn't account for the consumer as an advocate. Brand love, defined as the degree of passionate emotional attachment a consumer has for a particular brand (Carroll and Ahuvia 2006), does not say anything specific about the recommendation behavior of consumers.

In prior studies, the relationship between quality on the one hand and willingness to pay or brand loyalty on the other has been investigated. Perceived overall quality has been shown to have a positive influence on willingness to pay and consumers' purchase intentions (Agarwal and Rao 1996; Chang and Wildt 1994; Homburg et al. 2005; Taylor and Baker 1994). When customers experience elevated levels of satisfaction because of higher levels of perceived quality (Anderson and Sullivan 1993), they perceive to get more for what they paid and are thus willing to pay more for the brand (Homburg et al. 2005). Similarly, perceived quality has a positive effect on brand loyalty (McAlexander et al. 2003). Higher perceived quality increases the chance of repurchasing, as consumers tend to continue buying products with which they have good experiences. Since brand evangelism is closely related to brand loyalty, a positive relationship between perceived quality and brand evangelism can also be expected. These proposed relationships are summarized in hypothesis H1a and H1b.

> H1a: Perceived quality has a positive effect on consumers' willingness to pay a price premium.
>
> H1b: Perceived quality has a positive effect on consumers' brand evangelism.

8.3.2 Social Brand Value

Based on the sources of returns or profits that individuals get from social capital – social integration, symbolic or identity value and access to information – and the functions that a brand presents to consumers, we base the social brand value concept on three distinct underlying dimensions that present a source of value to the consumer: sense of community, social identity value and informational value. This means that we consider SBV as a second-order factor including those dimensions.

Sense of community. Sense of community is a brand's ability to allow consumers to develop a feeling of belonging to a group based on shared interests, rituals and traditions related to a specific brand (Kozinets 2002; McAlexander et al. 2002; Muniz and O'Guinn 2001). Literature on brand communities demonstrates that the consumption and preference of a brand helps to bring people together and can even lead to the forming of communities and tribes (Cova and Cova 2002; Muniz and O'Guinn 2001; Schau et al. 2009). Cova (1997) calls this ability the "linking" value of brands and argues that it has an increasing influence on consumer purchasing behavior. The networks established through brand communities and their embedded resources present social capital to those inside the networks. In order to be useful to the accumulation of social capital, brands must therefore be capable of bringing people together and must provide them with a feeling of social integration and community. This integration into a brand community can thereby take the form of an actual or imagined membership. Sense of community presents a means for consumers to build social ties and therefore accumulate social capital.

Social identity value. Social identity value refers to the identity-creating function of brands as promoters of social capital. Forming a personal identity and relating to others are among humankind's fundamental needs and behaviors (Douglas and Isherwood 1996; Toennis 1988). With respect to personal identity formation, research indicates that brands support consumers in their creation of self-concept and social identity (Ahuvia 2005; Belk 1988; Fournier 1998). "They (brands) serve as powerful repositories of meaning, purposively and differentially employed in the substantiation, creation, and (re)production of concepts of self in the marketing age" (Fournier 1998, p. 365). Brands are conceived as meanings shared by a group of people who use them as symbols in social interaction (Elliott 1994; Elliott and Wattanasuwan 1998; Richins 1994; Solomon 1983). Considering Boudieu's theory of capital, social capital is critical in determining the social space in which people can build their identity through interactions with their social networks. Since social ties around brands can enhance these networks, they help define the social space for interactions and thereby support identity formation through the accumulation of social capital. The social identity

8.3 Conceptual Model

value of brands is therefore based upon the determination of social space for identity creation and, thus, constitutes value for consumers.

Informational value. Informational value refers to informational benefits that interactions with other users about a brand can have for the consumer. Most consumer markets are characterized by asymmetric and imperfect information (Erdem and Swait 1998), which results in information gaps and hence certain risks for consumers. The exchange of information in social networks can be a mean to reduce the information imbalance in markets. Communication and interactions in networks around brands lead to the exchange and buildup of information – related or unrelated to the brand – within these networks. Being part of a network, an individual gets access to this pool of information and can utilize it. This pool of knowledge is consequently a value-enhancing part of brands for consumers. Therefore, the more brands are able to foster networks as repositories of information and knowledge around the brand, the more they add to consumers' social capital.

Although an overarching theory has been missing in literature so far, the existence of a social value of brands has been acknowledged. Various studies on brand communities (McAlexander et al. 2002; McAlexander et al. 2003; Muniz and O'Guinn 2001; Schau et al. 2009) found that consumers obtain some value-in-use from participating in these communities. More specifically, social connections enabled by these communities increase the value of the brand for consumers and companies through social ties based on interactions around the brand. In accordance with those findings, Franke and Piller (2004) showed that participation in communities increases the willingness to both pay and pay more (cp. Fuchs et al. 2010). Similarly, McAlexander et al. (2003) have demonstrated that brand community integration, a social value component of a brand, has a positive effect on the valuation of a brand and bears upon brand evangelism.

Based on our analysis of social capital theory and findings on the social value of brands, we expect the second-order factor of social brand value to have a positive effect on the valuation of a brand. Hypothesis H2a and H2b summarize this relationship.

H2a: Social brand value has a positive effect on consumers' willingness to pay a price premium.

H2b: Social brand value has a positive effect on consumers' brand evangelism.

Our final set of hypotheses aim to explain the impact of social brand value on the proposed direct relationships between perceived quality on the one side and willingness to pay (cp. Homburg et al. 2005) and brand loyalty or brand evangelism on the other side (McAlexander et al. 2003). Perceived quality as the subjective quality judgment of consumers influences interactions around a brand. High levels of perceived quality (as well as low levels) are going to spur communications around brands in social networks (Chen et al. 2011), which fosters the building of communities, identification with brands and the exchange of knowledge, i.e., higher levels of social brand value. Normal levels of perceived quality, in contrast, are not going to induce much interaction and are not going to have any significant effect on the social value of brands. Also, high quality has become a commodity for many brands and does not lead to differentiation anymore. As quality more and more becomes a basic requirement, it may not automatically trigger high levels of evangelism or raise consumers' willingness to pay (cp. Hoyer and Brown 1990). Because of those effects, we argue that perceived quality has an influence on social brand value and hence mediates the relationships between perceived quality on the one side and willingness to pay and brand evangelism on the other side. We propose in hypothesis H3a that perceived quality influences the second-order construct of social brand value positively and in hypotheses H3b and H3c that social brand value mediates the effects of perceived quality on the valuation of a brand.

H3a: Perceived quality influences the level of social brand value positively.

H3b: Social brand value mediates the relationship between perceived quality and willingness to pay a price premium.

H3c: Social brand value mediates the relationship between perceived quality and brand evangelism.

8.4 Empirical Study

8.4.1 Research Setting

An online questionnaire was developed to quantitatively explore the "social brand value" concept. We collected data from a representative online panel provided by Respondi, a leading German market research company. For their participation, panelists received points, which could later be traded for vouchers or other rewards. A prerequisite for participation in the study was the awareness of the brand presented in the questionnaire. In total, 1,301 questionnaires were completely filled out and returned to us. The 19 brands that have been selected for this study include software companies, social network brands, online-retailer, and consumer goods companies. All participants filled out the questionnaire for two of the 19 brands, which makes an average of 130 completed surveys per brand. The sample consisted of 51% male participants and 49% female participants. Concerning age, 28% of participants were between 14 and 30, 34% between 31 and 45, 25% between 46 and 60 and 14% above 60. For 25% of participants, brands had a high relevance, whereas for the rest, the relevance was either low (44%) or participants were neutral in respect to the relevance of brands (31%).

8.4.2 Measures

The questions and items used in our quantitative online survey were set up and refined based on the relevant literature. Table 5 shows all measures applied in this study. Except for demographic variables and the willingness to pay a price premium measure, five-point Likert-type scales were applied. To measure the construct of social brand value, we developed a second-order construct consisting of three sub-components: sense of community (two items), information value (two items) and identity value (two items). Sense of community was measured using two items adopted from Peterson et al.'s (2008) "sense of community scale." To measure the perceived informational value of the brands, we used two items from Mathwick et al. (2008). For the measurement of identity value, we adopted two items from Escalas and Bettman (2005) expressing the connectivity to the brand. To capture participants' subjective evaluation of the brands' quality, we employed three items from Pappu et al. (2005). The two items measuring consumers' brand evangelism were derived from the brand loyalty and positive word-of-mouth scale developed by Carroll and Ahuvia (2006). WTP was measured with one item asking participants how much more they were willing to pay for the brand in relation to an unbranded product. Similar one-item measures were used by Homburg et al. (2005) and Franke and Piller (2004) and are common when asking for consumers' willingness to pay.

8.4.3 Descriptive Analysis

Based on the survey results, we ranked the evaluated brands according to their perceived social value for participants (see Figure 6). We therefore added the scores brands received on the items for sense of community, identity value and informational value in the survey. The added scores were put together to compile a list which comparatively shows how different brands score in respect to their perceived social brand value.

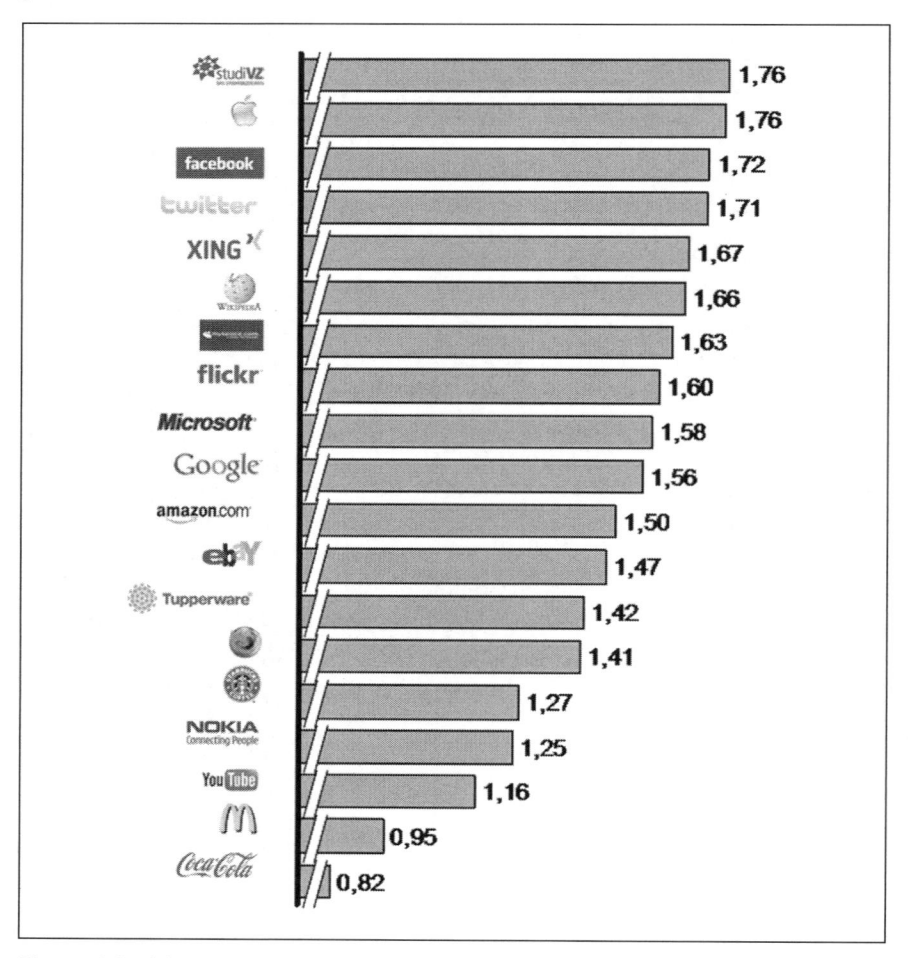

Brand	Score
StudiVZ	1,76
Apple	1,76
facebook	1,72
twitter	1,71
XING	1,67
Wikipedia	1,66
Amazon.com	1,63
flickr	1,60
Microsoft	1,58
Google	1,56
amazon.com	1,50
eBay	1,47
Tupperware	1,42
(logo)	1,41
(Starbucks)	1,27
NOKIA	1,25
YouTube	1,16
M (McDonald's)	0,95
Coca-Cola	0,82

Figure 6: Social Bramd Value Ranking

8.4 Empirical Study

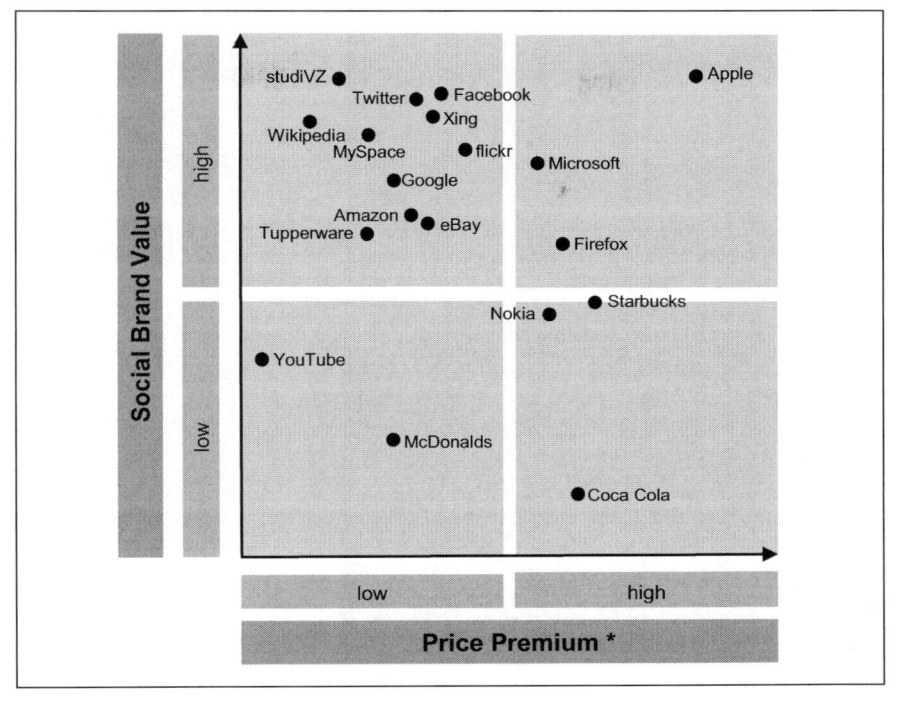

Figure 7: Social Brand Value – Price Premium Matrix

The resulting list demonstrates that there are significant differences in the perception of brands in light of their social value. Brands like studiVZ, Apple, and Facebook are strong in their overall social brand-value scores, whereas brands like Coca Cola, McDonalds, or Youtube are found at the end of the ranking. One explanation for this situation might of course be the difference in the offered products, as the top brands in our SBV ranking offer mainly high-involvement products, whereas Coca Cola and McDonalds offer convenience products. However, this result also indicates that those brands, in spite of their product category, are not really capable of engaging customers socially. The rather low rankings for brands like Flickr or YouTube indicate that purely distributing content online does not guarantee high SBV scores. Putting brands' SBV in relation to consumers' willingness to pay a price premium (see Figure 7) shows that there is some strong correlation between SBV and consumers willingness to pay a price premium for some brands, while for others it is not. Brands like Apple,

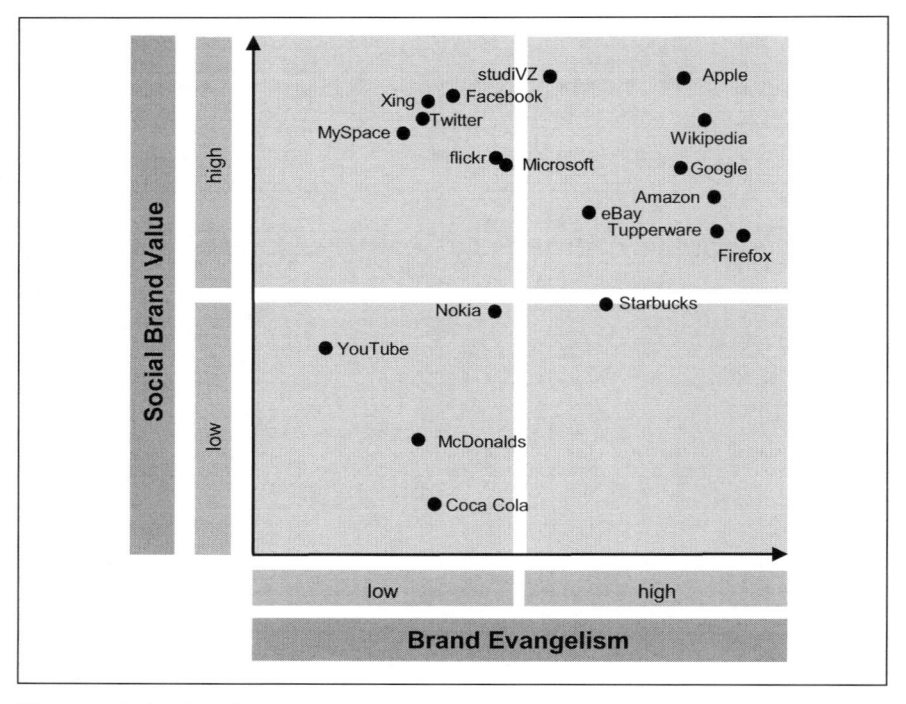

Figure 8: Social Brand Value – Brand Evangelism Matrix

Microsoft, Starbucks and Firefox, which are situated in the upper right corner of the matrix, seem to be able to transfer the social value they exhibit into higher prices. Brands like studiVZ, Facebook, Twitter and Wikipedia, although having a high social standing with consumers, are less capable of translating this into commercial profits.

When relating SBV to brand evangelism, the relationship seems to be less ambiguous (see Figure 8). Brands in the upper right hand corner have succeeded in establishing SBV and translating it into brand evangelism. Apple, Wikipedia, Google, Amazon and others have managed to create loyal consumers that are proactively advocating the brand. This indicates that they do have a strong standing with consumers and are capable of utilizing this advantage to induce evangelism. Overall, what can be drawn from this descriptive analysis is that SBV may have an influence on brands' overall value expressed through consumers' willingness to pay and brand evangelism. Further, SBV and its impact on the overall brand value may differ among brands. At this point, it is nevertheless unclear how the social brand value might influence the value of a brand in general. Our quantitative analysis aims to shed further light on the relationship between social brand value and overall brand equity.

8.4.4 Results

All measurement items as well as their psychometric properties are shown in Table 5.

All indicators show good factor loadings, and the respective factor reliabilities exceed the requirements (Bagozzi and Yi 1988). Convergent validity determined by the average variance extracted achieved satisfactory levels. Discriminant validity can be estimated by calculating the Fornell-Larcker-Ratio (Fornell and Larcker 1981), and the achieved value must not exceed 1. As expected, the three underlying facets of social brand value – identity value, information value and sense of community – exhibited problems with discriminant validity, as their Fornell-Larcker-Ratios were close to 1. We conducted a model comparison in order to check for the assumed underlying second-order factor called "social brand value" (SBV). As suggested by Bagozzi (1992), second-order models are especially useful when first-order factors are distinct but contain a significant shared variance. In order to test whether the second-order structure is also justified from an empirical point of view, we compared two models: one model, consisting of one single-merged, first-order factor that included all indicators previously used for the distinct factors "sense of community," "information value," and "identity value" and one model consisting of the second-order factor "social brand value" underlying these three dimensions. Following Burnham and Anderson (2004), AIC0 and BIC0 were used to compare the un-nested models and to evaluate the second-order structure. The analysis supports the second-order structure, as the difference measures AIC0, and BIC0 are all > 10 (First-order model: AIC 880, BIC 1062; Second-order model: AIC 423; BIC 616).

Method. Structural equation modeling was applied in order to test our conceptual framework and to explore the effect of social brand value (SBV) on the relationship between perceived quality on participants' willingness to pay a price premium for the brand as well as their brand evangelism. We further conducted the mediation test suggested by Baron and Kenny (1986) combined with a procedure suggested by Preacher and Hayes (2004) to test for the proposed mediating effect

Table 5: Measurement items used in the final model

Construct	Indicator	Factor loading	Factor reliability	AVE	Fornell-Larcker-Ratio
Brand Evangelism	I feel the need to tell others how good XXX is.	.92	.91	.84	.76
	If someone tries to decry XXX, I will tell him off unmistakably	.91			
Willingness to pay a price premium	How much more (in %) would you be willing to pay for XXX compared to an unbranded version:	1			
Quality	XXX offers very good quality	.89	.89	.73	.69
	The offer of xxx fits my needs	.83			
	XXX constantly works on improvements	.82			
Social Brand Value (2nd order)	Sense of Community	.97	.93	.82	.78
	Informational Value	.83			
	Identity Value	.92			
Sense of Community	Through XXX I feel like part of a community	.90	.86	.76	
	I take the opinion of other XXX users seriously	.84			
Social Identity Value	Being an XXX user is something special	.91	.93	.87	
	XXX is an important part of my identity	.94			
Informational Value	Through other XXX users I learn something new	.94	.92	.86	
	Through other XXX users I obtain valuable information	.92			

of SBV in the model. According to Baron and Kenny (1986), a variable functions as a mediator when (a) variations in the independent variable significantly account for variations in the presumed mediator, (b) variations in the mediator significantly account for variations in the dependent variable, and (c) when a previously significant relation between the independent and dependent variables is no longer significant, with the strongest demonstration of mediation occurring when this path is zero. Preacher and Hayes (2008; 2004) argue for a more direct test of the mediation effect by looking for a significant difference between the total effect between the independent and dependent variable and the direct effect between the two variables, which is controlled for the mediator. They thereby suggest the *distribution of the products* approach, which encompasses the calculation of the difference by means of an empirical approximation of the sampling distribution with a bootstrapping procedure.

Base Model. First, we analyzed the direct effects of quality on WTP and Evangelism (Figure 9). Multiple indices of model fit served for examining and evaluating the measurement models. The goodness-of-fit index (GFI), the adjusted goodness-of-fit index (AGFI), the comparative fit index (CFI), the normed fit index (NFI) and the root mean squared error of approximation (RMSEA) served as global and incremental fit indices. Satisfactory fits are obtained when the GFI, AGFI, CFI and NFI are greater than or equal to 0.9 and the RMSEA is less than or equal to 0.08. The results for the model fit were: χ^2 = 40.456, df = 7, p =

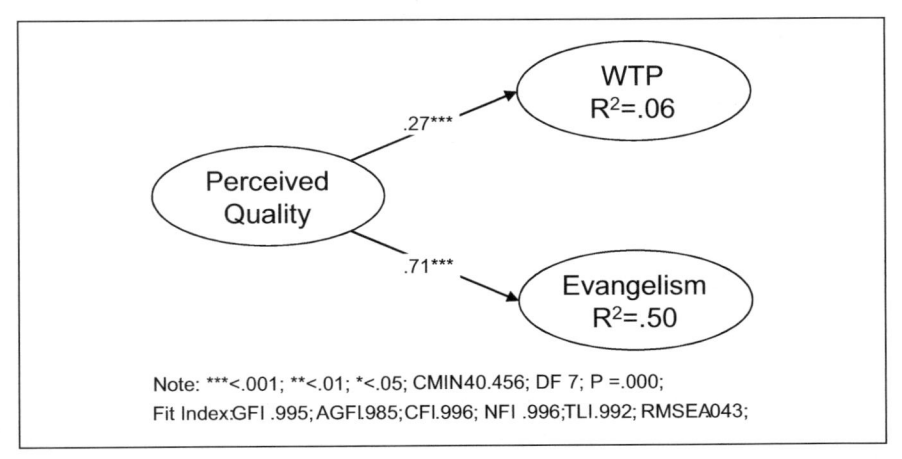

```
                                              ┌─────────────┐
                                    .27***    │    WTP      │
                                   ──────────▶│  R²=.06     │
                                              └─────────────┘
         ┌─────────────┐
         │  Perceived  │
         │   Quality   │
         └─────────────┘
                                              ┌─────────────┐
                                   .71***     │ Evangelism  │
                                   ──────────▶│  R²=.50     │
                                              └─────────────┘

Note: ***<.001; **<.01; *<.05; CMIN40.456; DF 7; P =.000;
Fit Index:GFI .995; AGFI.985; CFI.996; NFI .996; TLI.992; RMSEA043;
```

Figure 9: Structural model perceived quality and its effect on willingness to pay and brand evangelism

0.000, GFI = 0.995, AGFI = 0.985, CFI = 0.996, NFI = 0.996, and RMSEA = 0.043 indicating a satisfying overall fit to the data (see for example Browne and Cudeck 1993; Hu and Bentler 1999; Kline 1998).

The results given in Figure 5 show that quality has a significant influence on both WTP ($\gamma=.27^{***}$) and participants' brand evangelism ($\gamma=.50^{***}$). In total, quality explains 6% of WTP and 50% of participants' brand evangelism. Therefore, hypotheses H1a and H1b are fully supported.

Extended Model with SBV. Next, we amplified our model and introduced SBV in order to test its direct and mediating effects (Figure 6). The extended model also demonstrates a satisfying model fit. All fit measures meet the recommended range: $\chi^2 = 357.013$ df = 45, p = 0.000, GFI = 0.987, AGFI = 0.962, CFI = 0.988, NFI = 0.986, and RMSEA = 0.052.

Figure 10 portrays the results of the amplified structural equation model, assuming that SBV has additional effects on participants' WTP and brand evangelism. In total, SBV is able to raise the explained variance of WTP from $R^2 = .06$ to .20 and evangelism from $R^2 = .50$ to .75. The path analysis further reveals that SBV significantly impacts WTP ($\beta = .43^{***}$) as well as evangelism ($\beta = .59^{***}$). Hence, hypotheses H2a and H2b are fully supported.

SBV also fully mediates the impact of quality on WTP, as quality has a significant impact on SBV ($\gamma = .51^{***}$) and is able to account for a considerable amount in variance of SBV ($R^2 = .26$), changing the previously significant quality-WTP path to an insignificant relationship. Adding to that, there is a significant difference between the total effect of perceived quality on WTP and the direct effect between the two variables when controlling for SBV ($\gamma = .52$; Bootstrap estimates significantly [95 %] different from 0). This means that perceived quality does not automatically achieve a price premium. Only by providing social value to their users do brands attain an increased WTP. SBV can thus be interpreted to be a dominant predictor for both WTP and evangelism.

The impact of quality on evangelism further seems to be partially mediated by SBV, as the influence of quality on evangelism decreases and the overall explained variance of evangelism increases. However, the effect of quality on evangelism stays significant (Baron and Kenny 1986). Applying the direct test, results support the suggested mediating role of SBV in the perceived quality-brand evangelism relationship, as a significant difference between the total and the direct effect exists ($\gamma = .31$; Bootstrap estimates significantly [95%] different from 0). Therefore, hypotheses H3a, H3b and H3c are fully supported. In

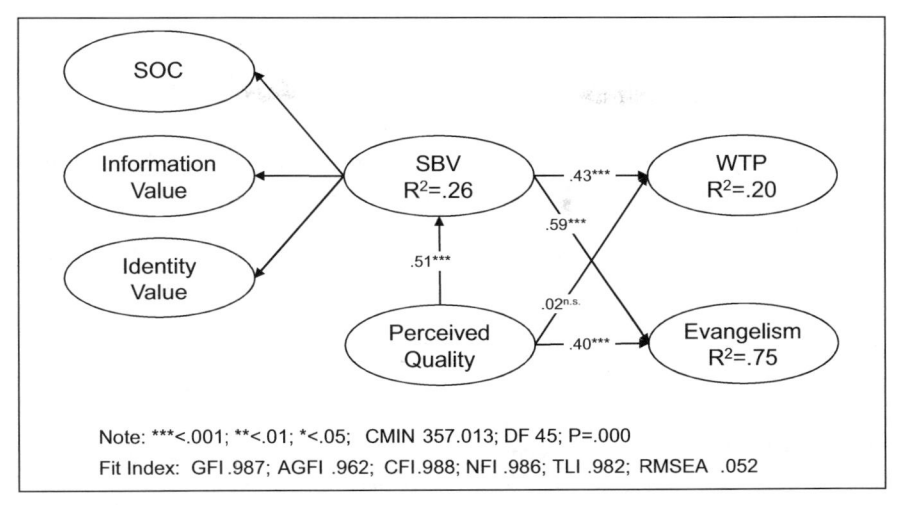

Figure 10: Amplified structural model including social brand value

addition to the full model consisting of 19 brands, we conducted a multi-group analysis to explore if the encountered effects differ between the 19 brands. No significant differences regarding the impact of SBV could be found among the different models, indicating that the effect of SBV is quite robust and may be applicable for all kinds of brands.

8.5 Discussion

In this article, we analyze the social value of brands from a consumer perspective. Based on an online survey with 1,301 participants, we develop a model around the social value of brands. In accordance with social capital theory, we show that social brand value (SBV) can be operationalized as a second-order factor using three dimensions: sense of community, informational value and identity value. Using structural equation modeling, we demonstrate that the second-order construct of SBV has a strong influence on brands' equity – in the form of consumers' willingness to pay a price premium – and on consumers' brand evangelism. Our analysis show that SBV mediates the direct relationships between perceived quality and price premium and between perceived quality and brand evangelism. Further, our model comparison among the different brands suggests that those effects are constant and do not significantly differ among brands. These results demonstrate that social aspects of a brand influence its perceived value for consumers. Networks of institutionalized relationships are valuable for those who have them (Bourdieu 1986). Resources that stem from these relationships build up social capital and help people form identities and realize goals. Brands nowadays play an important role in linking people together (Cova 1997) and thereby help build relationships and social capital. This study shows that consumers value the potential of brands as a linking device and as a source of social capital and thereby confirms the linking value (Cova 1997) and the social nature of brands (Muniz and O'Guinn 2001). Consumers are willing to pay a price premium for brands that offer social value to them and become active promoters of such brands. Our findings not only show the mere existence of social brand value but also its influence on consumers' decisions and how it contributes to brand equity. Thereby we confirm prior studies on the value-enhancing role of brand communities (McAlexander et al. 2002; Muniz and O'Guinn 2001; Schau et al. 2009) but enhance these findings in explaining the source of this value and in offering a conceptual framework to measure it.

In light of these results, a re-evaluation of existing brand equity measures seems to be worth considering. Brand equity is measured as an indicator of a brand's competitive position and serves to evaluate the success of marketing campaigns (Pappu et al. 2005). But brand equity measures, as widely used as they are today, do not account for social value aspects as important components of brand value (cp. Aaker 1991; Keller 1993; Pappu et al. 2005). Our research demonstrates the importance of social brand value as a component for consumers' valuation of brands. Hence, compiling a complete assessment of a brand's equity should include a measure for the social value of a brand. Especially in light of marketing activities in social media, such a measure may be essential for companies. Being active in social media requires brands to attract consumers by entertaining and by providing means for relationship-building among consumers, e.g., through enabling community building or promoting interactions. A social brand value measure as part of the brand equity construct could therefore provide guidance for brands in respect to the strategic and operational orientation of their social media activities.

The results from this study furthermore suggest that quality does not necessarily have a direct effect on consumers' willingness to pay a price premium, as demonstrated by former studies (cp. Homburg et al. 2005; Ruyter et al. 1998). Our study indicates that the effect of quality on willingness to pay for brands is fully mediated through social brand value. Providing high quality in products may no longer be a sufficiently differentiating characteristic of brands today; it has merely become a basic requirement. To make products stand out among the mass of offerings and to make consumers pay a price premium requires a socially inspired positioning of a brand. This finding constitutes the theoretical underpinning of the necessity of firms to be present in social media. The social kind of involvement with a brand that social media enables leads to brand equity and evangelism and provides strength for a brand that perceived quality alone cannot account for.

In addition to the widely described functional and symbolic benefits of brands (cp. Avery et al. 2010; Kapferer 2008; Keller 2008), this study demonstrates the social function brands have to fulfill. Consumers buy and use brands as well as interact with others around brands because of the social utility or value they gain from it. The social function of brands is becoming ever more important in the social media age where possibilities to interact become easier and more pervasive than ever.

Our study also provides some important practical implications for marketing and brand managers. Marketing managers have recognized the importance of social media engagements for their brands. However, the impact of these activeties and increased spending into social media campaigns were still unclear. This study presents an answer to this question as it demonstrates the importance of SBV for a company's brand and proposes that the power of a brand also lies within their potential to establish social ties among consumers. Consumers need to be attracted by a brand's presence in order to interact with and experience the brand. Only then, awareness, associations and the different dimensions of social capital can be influenced, which in further consequence leads to an increased willingness to pay a price premium and engage in brand evangelism. The descriptive results already indicated that brands like Apple, Microsoft, and Starbucks are able to score high on SBV and are also able to command high price premiums, while others like Tupperware and Amazon are not. One of the major challenges for brands may be to increase their social capital and also find some ways to transfer this into overall brand equity. Marketing managers, therefore, have to increase their branding capabilities in the social media space in order to successfully deal with user communities and support the brand communication among users in social networks.

We suggest managers track the social brand value of their brand in order to monitor the social capital generated by their marketing activities and media campaigns. Building value by creating relationships with social media activities is one component, but efforts will have to go beyond that. Brand-related interactions occur online as well as offline, and all branding efforts, therefore, have to account for the social value of brands. The framework introduced in this study may also serve as the basis for a tool to measure the social value of brands. The findings in this study request traditional brand equity approaches to recognize and capture the social nature of brands, especially considering the interactive social media age we are living in today.

8.6 Limitations and Future Research

To investigate the role of the social brand value construct for consumers, we chose three dimensions based on the concept of social capital: sense of community, social identity and informational value. Following social capital theory, these are the main factors contributing to the social value of a brand. Other dimensions, such as sources of meaningful relationship-building, bases for communication, or means for integration could qualify to further refine future versions of this construct.

Furthermore, to assess the effects of social brand value on brand equity, we measured consumers' *intended* willingness to pay and engage in brand evangelism and not their *actual* behavior. Further, it would be interesting to study how social brand value or social capital originates through social interactions and what firms would have to do exactly to be part of those interactions in social networks. Future research may explore how companies can support valuable brand interactions. Another interesting aspect to study would be the effects of negative attitudes towards a brand on its social brand value. In this study, we focused on positive attributes; however, negative reactions to a brand could also lead to social interactions and as a consequence to negative social capital and social brand value (Luedicke et al. 2010). Additionally, the role of word-of-mouth as an enabler of social capital could be studied. An interesting aspect may be to investigate how different types of word-of-mouth communication influence the creation of social capital.

Our theoretical derivation of SBV was grounded within social capital theory. The results from this study could further be analyzed from a cultural capital perspective. Holt (1998) argued that brands are modern citizen artists. Hence, future research could investigate the consequences of this notion for the social value of brands and how it relates to the social capital-based concept.

Our findings are also limited in that we investigated a certain geographical area and only included a limited number of brands. Nonetheless, this study contributes to a better understanding of the role of social brand value for consumers and clearly demonstrates its importance for the evaluation and conceptualization of brands.

9 The Impact of User Interactions in Social Media on Brand Awareness and Purchase Intention: The Case of MINI on Facebook

9.1 Introduction

The social media revolution has altered the communication landscape and has significantly impacted marketing communication. The growing importance of applications like Facebook, Youtube and others in consumers' lives has a growing influence on communication habits. With consumers spending more and more time in the social media realm, an increasing share of communication occurs within these new social network environments. In respect to marketing communication, this means that brand related interactions and exposure to marketing campaigns increasingly take place within social media (SM). The emerging communication setup has thereby transformed consumers from being passive participants in marketing to being active creators and influencers (Kozinets et al., 2008, Merz et al., 2009) and has shifted some power over brands directly to the consumer (Constantinides and Fountain, 2008). Bernoff and Li (2008) refer to this increasing influence of the user as "the growing groundswell of customer power" (p. 37) and a "cultural shift in a customer-centric direction" (p. 40). Traditional one-way communication in marketing has been transformed into a multi-dimensional two-way peer-to-peer communication reality (Berthon et al., 2008).

This new marketing communication reality presents new challenges and opportunities for companies as purchase decisions are increasingly influenced by social media interactions. People rely more than ever on their social networks when making those decisions (Hinz et al., forthcoming). Since an increasing part of this network is situated within the social media space and a large part of the communication within the network is happening in this space, SM platforms exhibit an important role in consumer decision making. Facebook and Co. become new key players for branding activities.

Nevertheless, outcomes of social media activities are still disputed in practice (Hoffman and Fodor, 2010). The effects of social media campaigns on consumers perception of products and brands as well as the effects on purchase decisions have yet to be better understood (Edelman, 2010, Barwise and Meehan, 2010). The potential drawbacks of SM activities like the spread of negative word of mouth and information overload causing disturbance and annoyance (McCoy et al., 2007), and the difficulties in measuring an added-value of such efforts have kept many marketing executives skeptical. Since brands cannot take the risk of being absent in such an influential communication channel, companies are investing increasingly into their social media activities (Divol et al., 2012).

This study therefore investigates how social media activities, in specific the Facebook appearance of a car manufacturer, affect the perception of brands, and ultimately influence the purchase decision process of consumers while considering the risk of creating annoyance. From a theoretical standpoint the results of this study contribute to our understanding of the value-enhancing potential of social media campaigns and demonstrate how the perception of brands is influenced through this new communication channel. For brand managers this study is of value, as it shows that social media activities do have a positive influence on brands as they support their management of the purchase process.

9.2 Consumers as Co-creators of Brands

Marketing literature in the last decade has undergone a shift towards a service-dominant logic (Vargo and Lusch, 2004). This logic puts the customer back into the center of marketing theory as it implies that the value of an offering (product or service) is defined and co-created with the consumer instead of being embedded in the output per se (Vargo and Lusch, 2008).

This new perspective on marketing is also reflected in contemporary understanding of brands. Brands are now viewed as an ongoing social process (Muniz and O'Guinn, 2001, Füller et al., 2012), whereby value is co-created in the interplay and negotiations of various stakeholders (Merz et al., 2009). Brand value is therefore "also co-created through network relationships and social interactions among the ecosystem of all the stakeholders" (Merz et al., 2009). Brand literature has evolved from a brand logic that viewed brands as simple markers of identification and value as embedded in goods determined by the value-in-exchange, to a new logic that views brands as being complex social phenomena (Holt, 2002, Kozinets, 2002, Pitt et al., 2006, Brown et al., 2003) and the value of the brands as its collectively perceived value-in-use (Franke and Piller, 2004, Schau et al., 2009).

The social nature of brands (Muniz and O'Guinn, 2001) and the relevance of relationships in co-creating brand value (McAlexander et al., 2002, Füller et al., 2012) enhance the importance of social media as a marketing channel. Social media favors relationship and community building as well as it promotes active engagements of consumers. The direct involvement social media enables in respect to the creation of brand value gives consumers ever more power to influence brands and posits challenges for brand managers' efforts to manage their brand. With the increasing relevance of social media platforms in the daily life of consumers, their marketing potential for brands increases as well. Therefore it has to be clarified where and how social media effects brand perceptions and brand related decisions of consumers.

9.3 Purchase Decision-making Process

Consumers make countless decisions every day and have to cope with increasing information overload. They therefore develop certain habits and "heuristics", which are shortcuts and "rules of thumb" used in decision making, to cope with this mental overload (Scammon, 1977, Jacoby et al., 1977, Jacoby, 1984). Brands are the most common rule of thumb in the contemporary marketplace. They facilitate many purchase decisions and offer reassurance as they connect current and future decisions to experiences, satisfactions and knowledge (Keller, 2008, Kapferer, 2008). Hence, brands play an important role in consumer decision-making and guide consumers in the process of making a purchase decision.

The consumer decision-making process comprises the various steps a consumer passes through when making a purchase-decision (Olshavsky and Granbois, 1979). This process encompasses all steps from the recognition of a need through the pre-purchase search for information about potential ways to satisfy the need, the evaluation of alternative options to the actual purchase and the post-purchase processes including experience and evaluation of the product.

Similar to the framework of the decision-making process are the "hierarchy of effects" (HOE) models in communication and advertising. Instead of describing the series of steps a consumer runs through when making a purchase decision, those models focus on the mental stages of the relationship of consumers with a specific product or brand (Vakratsas and Ambler, 1999, Ray, 1973). Hierarchy of

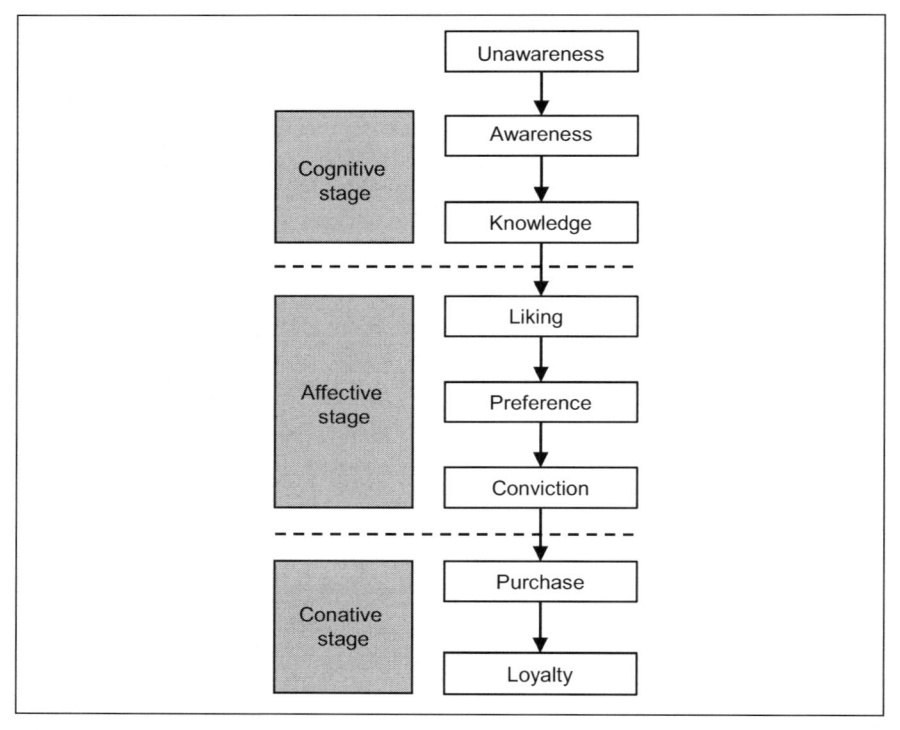

Figure 11: Hierarchy of effects (HOE) model

effects refers to the fixed order in which consumers perceive, process, and use advertising and other marketing communication information: first cognitively (thinking), second affectively (feeling), and third conatively (do) (Barry and Howard, 1990). This means that the consumer first attains awareness and knowledge about a product, subsequently develops positive or negative feelings towards the product and finally acts by buying and using or by rejecting and avoiding the product (Kotler and Bliemel, 2001). This kind of persuasive model argues for a hierarchical order in which things happen, with the implication that the earlier effects have a stronger impact on consumer's decision making (Vakratsas and Ambler, 1999). Based on this idea a variety of models has been proposed, differing in most cases only in nomenclature or order of effects (Barry and Howard, 1990, Vakratsas and Ambler, 1999).

The most well-known and widely applied hierarchy of effects model is AIDA, which consists of the purchase decision or attitude building phases awareness, interest, desire and action. Another widely recognized model is the one by Lavidge and Steiner (1961) (Figure 11). They included into their model the seven phases awareness, knowledge, liking, preference, conviction and purchase. At the beginning of the modeled process, the consumer is unaware of the brand. In the next phase he/she forms simple awareness. Subsequently, the consumer receives (e.g. through advertising or word-of-mouth) or searches for brand related information through which he/she builds knowledge about the brand offering. After the "thinking" stage, the consumer decides in the affective stage if she/he likes the product or not and builds preferences based on favorable or unfavorable attitudes towards the brand. At the end of the affective stage the consumer develops a conviction of the usefulness of the purchase, hence an intention to purchase. Even though not included in most HOE models (Barry and Howard, 1990, Vakratsas and Ambler, 1999, Smith et al., 2008), consumer loyalty and advocacy ideally follows the purchase phase.

Decisive for the sequence and flow of the single steps in the decision process is the involvement of consumers to the product or brand. According to Zaichkowsky (1985) involvement is defined as "a person's perceived relevance of the object based on inherent needs, values, and interests.", and depends on situational factors. In respect to the decision making process, involvement can influence the HOE in two ways. First, depending on the level of involvement consumers need differing amounts of time to go through the phases (Lavidge and Steiner, 1961). This means that for high involvement products like cars, consumers normally take longer when they for example search and process information and therefore need longer to get to the subsequent phase. Second, the level of involvement potentially also influences the sequence of the HOE stages (Kotler and Bliemel, 2001, Barry and Howard, 1990). With low involvement products the affective and conative phases could precede the cognitive one as consumers do not "think" when buying the product but build attitude after the purchase in the stage of using. Since the current study investigates the effects of the Facebook appearance of a car maker, the underlying processing conditions can be viewed as systematic and in line with the HOE sequence (Smith et al., 2008, Petty et al., 1983).

9.4 Conceptual Model and Hypothesis Development

For our conceptual model we choose three distinctive constructs to analyze how marketing activities in social media influence the consumer purchase decision-making process, modeled through the HOE (Figure 12). These include brand awareness, word-of-mouth and purchase intention. Fanpage involvement and annoyance serve as independent variables.

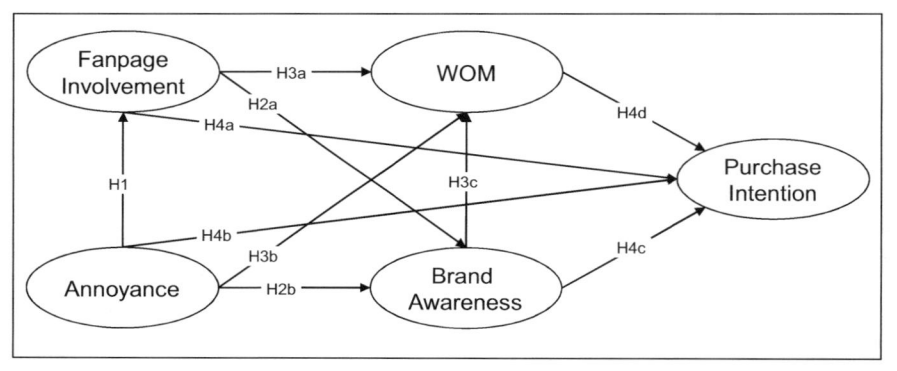

Figure 12: Conceptual model

Fanpage involvement. Fanpage involvement refers to a psychological attachment of participants to the community building efforts of a brand in social media environments, e.g. the creation of a Facebook fanpage of the brand (Kim et al., 2008, Morgan and Hunt, 1994). Fanpage involvement can be viewed as the active and psychological involvement of a consumer with the social media activities of a brand.

Annoyance. When consumer commitment and enjoyment of social media content by companies or brands turns into annoyance, the consumer turns away quickly. Social media marketing is considered to be less intrusive, and thus less annoying, than some traditional marketing techniques since consumers have more control over their exposure to the content. Therefore companies – using this marketing channel – have to be diligent in entertaining consumers with their marketing efforts in order to keep their attention.

Whereas enjoyment has been referred to be a pleasurable response to the exposure to (entertainment) media (Tamborini et al., 2010), annoyance is the unpleasant emotional reaction to subjective overexposure to a certain kind of media. Annoyance may result from unwanted exposure to advertising (McCoy et al., 2007) or intrusive direct marketing (Lee and McGowan, 1998). Therefore, companies have to be diligent in approaching consumers in social media in order to avoid annoyance. Social media content that disturbs and ultimately annoys consumers is not only ineffective from a marketing perspective, but can even have negative effects for the brand. We propose:

> H1: Annoyance with the content of a brand page has a negative effect on BPC.

Brand awareness (BA). Two of the main purposes in branding are the "labeling" of a product through marketing means and making consumers aware of the label. The created BA "is related to the strength of the resulting brand node or trace in memory, as reflected by consumers' ability to identify the brand under different conditions" (Keller, 2008). In other words brand awareness refers to the strength of a brand's presence in consumers' minds.

The importance of brand awareness in consumer decision-making has three major reasons (Keller, 1993). First, it is important that consumers think about a brand when making a purchase decision within the product category of the brand. Raising brand awareness increases the likelihood that a brand will be a part of the consideration set, which is the basket of brands, which are considered when making a purchase decision (Baker et al., 1986, Chakravarti et al., 2003). Considering the HOE, brand awareness represents the first phase and the prerequisite that consumers reach the subsequent stages. Second, brand awareness can influence decisions about brands in the consideration set, even if there are basically no other associations with the brand. It has been shown that consumers tend to adopt a decision rule to purchase familiar and well known brands (Roselius, 1971, Jacoby et al., 1977). Especially in low involvement situations it has been demonstrated that basic brand awareness alone may be sufficient to influence the choice of a brand, even if well-formed attitudes are missing (Hoyer and Brown, 1990, Bettman and Park, 1980). Third, brand awareness influences the formation and strength of brand associations making up brand image. A necessary condition for consumers to create associations with the brand is the presence of the brand in consumers' minds. The strength of the presence or mental node decides how easily different kinds of information can become attached to the brand (Keller, 2008).

Brand awareness is created by anything that causes the consumer to experience the brand –advertising, promotion, publicity, public relations, etc. Social media represents one way to expose consumers to the brand and thereby create brand awareness. It follows that the more actively consumers engage with the social media activities of a brand, i.e. the higher the fanpage involvement is, the higher the awareness of the brand is. A negative relationship can be expected between annoyance and brand awareness. We state:

> H2a: Fanpage involvement has a positive effect on brand awareness.
>
> H2b: Annoyance with the content of a brand page has a negative effect on brand awareness.

Word of mouth (WOM). WOM is a naturally occurring phenomenon in consumer behavior (Kozinets et al., 2010). It refers to all kinds of interpersonal communication (positive and negative) about a company, brand or product between a receiver and a communicator, who is perceived as non-commercial (Arndt, 1967, Goyette et al., 2010). WOM serves as one source of information for consumers in the purchase-decision making process as it provides information on product performance and the social and psychological consequences of a potential purchase decision (Mooradian et al., 2012, Brown et al., 2007). Since consumers are familiar with the source of WOM, the received information is considered to be more reliable, credible, and trustworthy (Solomon, 2011). As a consequence, WOM as a source of information is more effective in influencing consumers' decision-making than other marketing communication channels (Katz and Lazarsfeld, 1955, Kozinets et al., 2010). WOM includes positive as well negative information on a product or brand

In respect to the HOE model, WOM has a strong influence on the cognitive and affective stages, especially knowledge and liking, and is a potential consequence of the loyalty phase. Especially loyalty, and similarly brand evangelism (Füller et al., 2012), is closely related to WOM. When consumers are loyal to a product or brand they tend to talk about it and thereby spread (positive) WOM. They can even become ambassadors of a brand as they actively show and convince others of their object of loyalty. Hence, WOM plays an important role in the HOE attitude model as an input and output component.

The accessibility, reach, and transparency of the internet has extended consumers' options to gather information and engage in WOM (Hennig-Thurau et al., 2004). Social media applications present an option to spread WOM and expose consumers to WOM. Whereas the speed of classic oral word-of-mouth communication used to be rather slow, social media and its immediate reach of literally millions of consumers has increased the diffusion of WOM substantially. The desire to communicate to others, which includes negative and positive WOM, is one of the main reasons to use social media.

The degree of involvement with social media applications like Facebook fanpages, i.e. the level of Fanpage involvement, as well as brand awareness could therefore be an indicator of positive WOM activities. Since brand awareness is the first step in the HOE, it also is logically the first and most important prerequisite of WOM. It follows that the stronger a presence of a brand in consumers' minds is, the likelier is it for consumers to think and talk about a brand. Annoyance can be expected to have the opposite effect on positive WOM. We propose:

> H3a: Fanpage involvement has a positive effect on positive on WOM activities.
>
> H3b: Annoyance with the content of a brand page has a negative effect on WOM activities.
>
> H3c: Higher levels of brand awareness have a positive effect on WOM activities.

Purchase intention. At the end of the affective stage of the HOE model, consumers build an intention to purchase the brand (Lavidge and Steiner, 1961). Purchase intention refers to the mental stage in the decision making process where the consumer has developed an actual willingness to act toward an object or brand (Wells et al., 2011, Dodds et al., 1991). Marketing communication's primary goal is to get consumers to form an intention to purchase the marketed product. Hence, the effectiveness of social media activities of firms will be measured against this goal. SM should therefore positively influence consumers purchase intention (Keller, 2008, Kapferer, 2008). In line with the HOE, we argue that:

> H4a: BPC has a positive effect on consumers' purchase intention.
>
> H4b: Annoyance with the content of a brand page has a negative effect on purchase intentions
>
> H4c: Brand awareness has a positive effect on purchase intentions.
>
> H4d: WOM has a positive effect on purchase intentions.

9.5 Empirical Study and Analysis

9.5.1 Data Collection

To answer our research questions and test our hypotheses, a study was set up in cooperation with the car brand MINI. A link to an online questionnaire was broadcasted through a posting on the MINI Facebook brand page notifying all visitors of the German speaking MINI Facebook brand page members. After purification of missing values 311 cases remained for further analysis. 51% of the respondents were male and 49% female. 50% of the respondents were aged between 14 and 28 and 32% were aged between 29 and 39. Only 18% of the respondents were over 40, while the average age was 30.4. 69% of the respondents already owned a MINI, 81% declared themselves as fans of MINI, 36% stated to be fans of cars in general and 6% of all participants are employees at MINI.

9.5.2 Measures

The questions and items used were set up and refined based on literature and measured on seven point Likert-scale. *Fanpage involvement* was measured using six adapted items from Ellison et el. (2007) and Kim et al. (2008), capturing the extent to which participants actively engage in and are emotionally connected to activities on the MINI Facebook brand page. *Word-of-mouth* (WOM) was captured by four items slightly adapted from Hennig-Thurau et al. (2004). *Brand awareness* was measured through three items adopted from Yoo et al. (2000). We thereby did not only measure the awareness of the brand MINI itself but also of the range of MINI models. *Annoyance* was captured with three items measuring the acceptance of shared content while *purchase intention* was captured by three items in accordance with the MINI sales funnel. To assure that participants' involvement with the Facebook fanpage influenced the variables, we specifically asked for the effect of the experience with and participation in the MINI fanpage. The questions therefore all started with the phrase "because I'm a member of the MINI Facebook fanpage, …" so that participants related the questions directly to the Facebook activities of MINI.

9.5.3 Results

To test our hypotheses, we applied structural equation modeling with AMOS 18. A maximum likelihood estimation was run, which yielded a satisfying overall fit of the model CMIN/DF 1.62; GFI .931; CFI .971; NFI .928; AGFI .904; RMSEA .045 (see for example Hu and Bentler, 1999; Kline, 1998; Browne and Cudeck, 1993). The psychometric properties of the latent constructs and the wording of the items, are displayed in Table 6 and indicate an appropriate structure. All indicators have good factor loadings and the respective factor reliabilities exceed the required reliability in structural equation modeling of 0.6 (Bagozzi and Yi, 1988). The average variance extracted from the constructs can be judged as satisfactory with values over 0.5 (except for purchase intention with 0.46 still tolerable) and thus, the convergent validity of the constructs can be seen as fulfilled (Hair et al., 2006). Discriminant validity can be estimated by calculating the Fornell-Larcker-Ratio (Fornell and Larcker, 1981), which must not exceed 1.

Concerning the path analysis our model Figure 13 displays the results of our analysis. Annoyance is found to negatively and significantly impact fanpage involvement (−.27***) thereby supporting H1. Fanpage involvement positively influences brand awareness (.40***) and WOM (.35***). Hence, H2a and 3a are fully supported. No influence of annoyance on brand awareness (−.06n.s.) could be found, but results show that annoyance negatively impacts WOM (−.09†). While no support is provided for H2b, our results support H3b. Further, no relationship can be found between brand awareness and WOM providing no support for H3c. Finally, purchase intention is found to be positively and significantly influenced by fanpage involvement (.23**), and by brand awareness (.25**), however no negative impact was found for annoyance (.00n.s.) or positive impact could be found for WOM (.15n.s.). Hence, only hypotheses 4a and 4c are supported. In total our model is able to explain 7% of variance in fanpage involvement, 18% of variance in awareness, 61% in WOM, and 28% in purchase intention.

Table 6: Psychometric properties of the scales

Construct	Item	Loading	Mean (SD)	CR	AVE	FLR
Fanpage Involvement	*As a member of the MINI Facebook fanpage*			.85	.50	.75
	… I get informed about MINI news daily	.74	3.30 (1.86)			
	… I feel as a part of the MINI-Facebook Community	.75	3.76 (1.82)			
	… have a close relationship to other MINI FB-Fans	.64	4.55 (2.07)			
	… I participate in activities on the page very often	.57	3.27 (1.84)			
	… I miss something if I do not visit regularly	.81	2.63 (1.71)			
	… it is fun for me to inspire others about MINI	.64	1.97 (1.02)			
Word of Mouth	*Because I'm a member of the MINI Facebook fanpage*			.91	.67	.73
	… I talk very positive about MINI	.65	5.03 (2.02)			
	… can recommend MINI to my friends and relatives	.79	4.60 (2.12)			
	… I try win my friends and relatives as MINI fans	.82	3.28 (2.09)			
	… it is fun for me to inspire others about MINI	.90	4.49 (2.18)			
Brand Awareness	*Because I'm a member of the MINI Facebook fanpage*			.88	.72	.68
	… I have no difficulties to remember MINI	.70	4.15 (2.19)			
	… know all MINI models	.93	4.30 (2.16)			
	… I can distinguish the different MINI Model	.92	4.16 (2.27)			
Purchase Intention	Because I'm a member of the MINI Facebook fanpage			.72	.46	.52
	… I plan to buy a MINI	.60	2.80 (2.11)			
	… I have arranged a test ride.	.70	1.74 (1.49)			
	… I have bought a MINI	.71	1.95 (1.87)			
Annoyance	*I think it is disturbing if…*			.82	.61	.48
	… my wall is overloaded with MINI Topics	.85	3.65 (2.11)			
	… the same MINI topic is forward multiple times	.72	4.02 (1.49)			
	… MINI posts product ads all the time	.77	3.32 (1.87)			

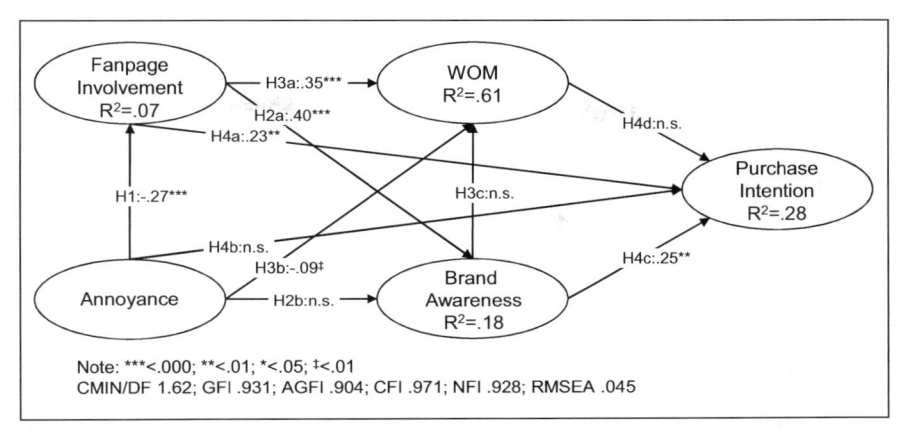

Figure 13: Model

9.6 Discussion and Implications

In this article, we analyze the influence of brands' social media activities and participants' social media involvement on the purchase decision process of consumers. Our findings demonstrate that engagement with a Facebook fanpage has positive effects on consumers' brand awareness, WOM activities and purchase intention. Results further indicate that annoyance with the fanpage leads to negative effects in respect to the overall commitment and involvement to the fanpage and WOM.

Our research shows that social media activities indeed affect the purchase decision making process. We could thereby demonstrate that they influence the different phases described in the hierarchy of effects model (Smith et al., 2008, Petty et al., 1983). Social media activities influence all three mental stages: the cognitive phase, the affective stage, and the cognitive stage. The HOE model thereby represents a possible mental process that a consumer goes through when making a purchase decision. The real process will most of the time deviate from the one modeled by the HOE. The described phases, in one form or the other, are still part of every decision making process, independent of product category, time or prior experience. Our findings thereby indicate that social media is a viable and relevant marketing communication channel for brands.

Based on this, our study supports prior findings that social media content influences the economic outcome of brands (Zhu and Zhang, 2010) and that WOM and social media are inextricable forms of marketing (Kozinets et al.,

2010). We extend these prior findings in showing their applicability in respect to the Facebook presence of a brand. We thereby also applied a more holistic approach to the impact of social media activities for brands as we studied the whole purchase decision process and not just specific outcomes like sales or purchase intention.

With postmodern information overload, annoyance has become an issue for all marketing communication efforts. When consumers get annoyed by the marketing activities of a brand, they can quickly turn against the brand, e.g., by not considering the brand when making a purchase or by spreading negative word of mouth. Social media in general is considered to be less intrusive than other marketing communication efforts as consumers can more easily decide the extent of exposure to marketing content. Nevertheless, social media fanpages could easily annoy fans by posting too much and thereby spam the message boards of users. Annoyance in respect to social media content is an underresearched area. More research is needed to better understand the effects of annoyance in online and social media environments and to investigate more what causes annoyance in a social media environment. This would be an important contribution to the explanation of consumer behavior in respect to social media marketing and to the understanding of the effect of social media brand activities on purchase behavior. Our results indicate that annoyance with social media content has negative effects on the evaluation of brands in the purchasing process and reduces WOM. This study is thereby a first attempt into explaining potential effects of social media annoyance on consumer purchase behavior. It thereby also indicates, that it is often not just the amount of negative of positive WOM (Kozinets et al., 2010, Liu, 2006) that counts but has to be considered as well is the level of annoyance that social media appearances cause with consumers.

From a managerial perspective, the findings in this study underpin the relevance of social media for brand management. While managers may still doubt the usefulness of social media involvements, our study points in the direction of social media as an important and integral part of the marketing communication strategy.

The positive effects of consumers' social media engagements on brand awareness, WOM activities and purchase intention are strong arguments for the relevance of social media in respect to the management of brands. Social media shouldn't be something companies engage in because everyone else is doing or because it is thought to be important for a modern and open image of brands. Also, brand managers today use social media activities mostly as means to gather information and learn about consumers and their attitude towards the products and the brand. Those reasons to be active in social media are relevant, but managers have to realize that social media is a viable marketing instrument as well, which, if applied correctly, can have positive economic effects for the brand and the company.

With respect to annoyance, this study points to a thus far neglected topic in association with marketing efforts in social media. When discussing the downside of social media and user-generated content, the focus has mostly been on the impact of negative WOM (Liu, 2006, Kozinets et al., 2010). Marketing managers, when planning social media activities, should evaluate annoyance issues since these could easily deteriorate any efforts made and could lead to negative outcomes for the brand. Social media has unique dynamics and users react sensitive to its content. Managers need to understand those dynamics and the users within social media environments and need to respect the social media norms of engagement. This understanding is vital for having long term marketing success in social media.

9.7 Limitations and Outlook

This study also has limitations that lead to future research opportunities. Our study was conducted with the Facebook fanpage of MINI and hence only members of this fanpage were included in our sample and the provided results stem from a single fanpage. Therefore a sampling bias may affect our findings. Other brand pages from different product categories should be investigated in the future.

Also, other factors influencing the purchase decision process could be included to refine the model and deepen the understanding of social media's influence on the decision-making process. Another interesting aspect in context of social media and the purchase decision process is the viability of the HOE. Especially the sequence of the phases should be analyzed and possibly revised if it is altered by social media involvement. This could lead to a new understanding of our communication and information processing habits in respect to social media and other new forms of media.

Annoyance is a highly relevant topic for brands in respect to social media. Longer term experience with this new form of media is missing. More research is needed to further investigate what causes annoyance and how it can be avoided. Similarly, more research is needed to better understand the causes and effects of social media related enjoyment and entertainment on brand attitudes.

10 Contributions and Implications

10.1 Theoretical Implications

This thesis aims at contributing to marketing and branding literature by shedding light on the impact and consequences of user-generated content and social media on brand perceptions and marketing management. The theoretical contributions of this thesis thereby include describing and defining UGBs in virtual worlds, explaining SBV and authenticity as an important value-component of UGBs, demonstrating the value-enhancing potential of a brand's social nature as well as underpinning some essential arguments for branding in social media.

While the existence of UGBs has been described in previous studies (cp. Füller et al. 2008; Pitt et al. 2006), this thesis represents the first attempt to describe user-generated brands in a virtual world environment and introduces a framework of their characteristics. The findings thereby deepen our understanding on how UGBs emerge and differ from corporate brands. In the age of social media, the differentiation between UGBs and corporate brands might diminish over time, but some fundamental differences are likely to remain. The unintentional nature of this type of entrepreneurship in combination with the unique understanding of the environment will be difficult for corporations to imitate.

In describing and explaining authenticity as an important characteristic for UGBs, this thesis contributes to our understanding of authenticity as a value driver for brands. Our findings show that authenticity – the encapsulation of what consumers perceive as genuine, real and/or true (Beverland et al. 2010; Gilmore and Pine 2007) – is a vital component for UGBs. They have an inherent authentic image, as they utilize their naturally evolved understanding of the product, environment, and its users to more closely tailor products and brands to the needs and desires of users (cp. Holt 2002). Authenticity, from a consumer perspective, derives its importance today from the shift towards a more experience driven economy (Gilmore and Pine 2007). In combination with an increase in technology-driven interactions, a postmodernistic and socially constructed reality and a loss of trust in established institutions, an increasingly unreal world, filled with deliberately and sensationally staged experiences, drives consumers to search for products that they perceive as real, original, sincere, genuine – in short, authentic (Gilmore and Pine 2007; Henderson and Bowley 2010). Similarly, the loss of traditional sources of meaning and self-identity caused by postmodernism (Arnould and Price 2000) and the standardization and homogenization in the marketplace (Thompson et al. 2006) have been identified as drivers for the active and adept appropriation of authenticity in consumption patterns. Hence, being perceived as authentic could prove to be an important competitive advantage.

Furthermore, this thesis empirically tests and supports the notion of a social nature or value of brands. Networks of institutionalized relationships are valuable for those who have them (Bourdieu 1986). Resources that stem from these relationships make up social capital and help people form identities and realize goals. Brands nowadays play an important role in linking people together (Cova 1997; Cova et al. 2007) and thereby help build relationships and social capital. This study shows that consumers value the potential of brands as a linking device and as a source of social capital and thereby confirms the linking value (Cova 1997) and the social nature of brands (Muniz and O'Guinn 2001). Consumers are, for the most part, only subconsciously aware of this potential but nevertheless value it and are therefore, among other reasons, drawn towards brands, are willing to pay a price premium for brands, and become active promoters of brands. Hence, this thesis not only shows the existence of social brand value but also demonstrates its value for consumers and how it contributes to brand equity. These findings thereby suggest a re-evaluation of existing brand equity measures. Brand equity is measured by firms as an indicator of a brand's competitive position and serves to evaluate the success of marketing campaigns (Pappu et al. 2005). However, brand equity measures today do not account for social value aspects as important components of brand value (cp. Aaker 1991; Keller 1993; Pappu et al. 2005). It can be inferred that brand equity literature needs to consider the inclusion of this value component in its models. To compile a complete assessment of a brand's equity necessitates the integration of a measure for the social value of a brand. Based on the social brand value concept introduced in this thesis, a social brand value component should be incorporated into the construct of brand equity. This would facilitate a more holistic view on the value potential of a brand.

In its attempt to test the value-enhancing role of brand's social value, the results of this thesis also indicate that quality does not necessarily have a direct effect on brand value. This finding thereby contradicts other studies that have argued for an effect of perceived quality on consumers' willingness to pay (cp. Homburg et al. 2005; Ruyter et al. 1998). Quality might no longer be a sufficiently differentiating characteristic of brands today; it has merely become a basic requirement. To make products stand out and to increase consumers' willingness to pay asks for a socially inspired positioning of a brand. This finding furthermore constitutes the theoretical underpinning of the necessity of firms to be present in social media. The social kind of involvement with a brand that social media enables provides strength for a brand that perceived quality alone cannot account for.

Moreover, this research also contributes to literature on consumer decision-making and branding as it provides evidence that social media marketing influences the decision-making process of consumers and consumers' brand attitudes. Hierarchy of effects models refer to the order in which consumers perceive, process, and use marketing information related to a potential purchase (Lavidge and Steiner 1961). With this thesis it could be shown that social media activities affect the purchase decision-making process as they influence all three mental stages a consumer runs through, as follows: first, the cognitive phase, as brand awareness is build; second, the affective stage, as WOM is an important source for the formation of preferences towards a product or brand; and third, the conative stage, as the intention to purchase is directly affected by the commitment to a fanpage and indirectly by brand awareness and WOM. Our findings thereby indicate that social media is a viable and relevant marketing communication channel for brands, as its influencing power is similar to traditional communication channels like advertising in respect to the investigated dimensions. Hence, given the rapid growth and increasing consumer acceptance of social media, the relevance of this channel for brand management is likely to further increase.

In addition, the results also indicate potential dangers and shortcomings of social media efforts. With postmodern information overload, annoyance has become an issue for all marketing communication efforts. When consumers get annoyed by a brand's marketing activities they can quickly turn against the brand, e.g., by not considering the brand when making a purchase decision or by spreading negative WOM. Especially with social media, diligence in how to approach consumers is required from firms, as consumers are free to decide what they want to experience or what they want to be exposed to. Results indicate that annoyance with social media content negatively effects the evaluation of brands in the purchasing process.

10.2 Managerial Implications

From a managerial perspective, the findings in this thesis yield various important implications. First, it gives practitioners insights on important brand management issues in virtual worlds, which might also be applicable for social media in general. One of the acute problems corporate brands are currently dealing with is how to best use virtual worlds or social media in the co-creation process of brand meaning. Most companies are already active in social media, but best practices have yet to be established. Based on the findings about UGBs and branding in social media we developed five recommendations for brand management in virtual worlds and other social media application: (1) engage and involve customers and let them inspire you; (2) understand users and their environment; (3) word-of-mouth is key to promotion; (4) enable community building; and (5) be authentic in what you do.

Second, this thesis provides a rationale for marketing activities within social media and underpins the relevance of social media for brand management. The studies show that social media marketing, if conducted diligently, can lead to higher purchase intentions and brand evangelism and is important in creating social brand value. Hence, social media efforts do pay off and need to be taken seriously by marketers and brand managers. Even though increasing amounts of investments pour into marketing campaigns within this communication channel, managers are still unsure about the reasons for social media's importance for their brands. The results presented may help managers to better understand the role social media can play for their brands and to comprehend where the value-enhancing potential with social media lies. The positive effects of consumers' social media engagements on their purchase decision-making are one strong argument. Another argument is the proposed power of social media activities to generate brand related social capital, i.e., SBV, through establishing social ties among consumers. SBV increases brand equity and presents an indicator for the marketing performance of companies. However, to profit from social media, simply having presences is insufficient. Consumers need to be attracted by a brand's presence in order to interact with and experience the brand. Only then awareness, associations, and other brand dimensions can be influenced, which in further consequence leads to an increased value of the brand.

Finally, this thesis provides insights for managers on a potentially challenging phenomenon for established brands – user-generated brands. For example, various studies have shown the relevance of authenticity for consumer's self-conception in consumption (Holt 2002; Kates 2004; Thompson et al. 2006). The higher perceived authenticity demonstrated in this thesis indicates the possibility that user-created brands could conquer a market niche where consumers have a high need for authentic brands. This study thereby also demonstrates where commercial brands have potential shortcomings and could improve their branding efforts. Practitioners could learn valuable lessons from UGBs in how to establish authenticity or tailor products closer to the needs of consumers.

11 Limitations and Future Research

In closing, several important key areas for further research are identified which are not only suggested by the findings but also address limitations inherent in the research presented in the course of this thesis.

First, because of the unique nature of specific social media applications (e.g., Facebook, Second Life) the transferability of findings to other social media environments has to be treated with caution. Further research should investigate various other social media environments to build an overarching understanding of user-generated brands in those environments. As social media is a rather new form of "mass" media, only experience will show which applications will dominate the future of UGC and will have a lasting impact in brand management., especially with respect to UGBs.

Second, we have focused on a static description of UGBs, e.g., by analyzing and describing the characteristics of UGBs. As the creation of brand meaning involves various stakeholders and occurs as a dynamic process (Merz et al. 2009), future research should take on a procedural perspective to study the creation and emergence of UGBs and should investigate the co-creation process of brand meaning to get a more holistic picture on the phenomenon (cp. Diamond et al. 2009).

Third, to assess the relevance of brands' social nature for the valuation of brands, this thesis focused on measuring consumers' intended behavior and not their actual behavior. Future research could deploy different research designs, e.g., experiments or auctions, which enable the elicitation of consumer action instead of their opinion. Research on actual behaviors would further validate the results and could describe the effects of interest in more detail.

Fourth, it would be interesting to study how social brand value or social capital originates through social interactions. The social nature of brands has only been acknowledged recently and this thesis represents the first attempt to measure the social brand value and show its effects on brand equity. It would be interesting to study different marketing strategies that commercial brands deploy to strengthen their social brand value. This would also provide insights into what firms would need to do to become part of interactions in social networks in order to build SBV.

Finally, this thesis has investigated authenticity and sympathy as drivers of UGBs potential competitive advantage. Future research should try to focus on different dimensions of a brand in order to get a more complete view on potential advantages that UGBs might exhibit to consumers in comparison to corporate brands.

Overall, research on the consequences and prerequisites of marketing and branding with social media is only in the early stages of its development. The future will show, which impact the social media revolution, we are seeing today, will have on consumers' and marketers' lives. Studies across various social media applications and theoretical areas will have to shed more light on potential marketing strategies and consumers reactions to them.

User-generated content and user-generated brands represent a promising new field of study. Even though this thesis provides some insights, many questions remain unanswered to date. The insights provided in this research and the new questions stimulated by this work wish to inspire other scholars to further explore the interesting phenomenon of user-driven and socially inspired brand creation. In light of the emergence of new information and communication technologies and social software application, it is reasonable to expect that in the future UGC and UGBs will attract even more attention by both scholars and practitioners.

12 References

Aaker, David A. (1991). Managing Brand Equitiy. New York, NY: The Free Press.

Aaker, David A. (1996). Measuring brand equity across products and markets. California Management Review, 38 (3), 102-20.

Aaker, David A. and Joachimsthaler, E. (2000). Brand Leadership. Free Press, New York.

Aaker, J., Fournier, S., and Brasel, S. A. (2004). When Good Brands Do Bad. Journal of Consumer Research, 31 (1), 1-16.

Agarwal, Manoj K. and Vithala R. Rao (1996). An empirical comparison of consumer-based measures of brand equity. Marketing Letters, 7 (3), 237-47.

Ahuvia, A. C. (2005). Beyond the Extended Self: Loved Objects and Consumers' Identity Narratives. Journal of Consumer Research, 32 (1), 171-184.

Anderson, Eugene W. and Mary W. Sullivan (1993). The Antecedents and Consequences of Customer Satisfaction for Firms. Marketing Science, 12 (2), 125-43.

Arakji, R. Y. and Lang, K. R. (2008). Avatar Business Value Analysis: A Method for the Evaluation of Business Value Creation in Virtual Commerce. Journal of Electronic Commerce Research, 9, 207-218.

Arndt, J. (1967). Role of Product-Related Conversations in the Diffusion of a New Product. Journal of Marketing Research (JMR), 4, 291-295.

Arnould, E. J., and Price, L. L. (2000). Authenticating acts and authoritative performances: questing for self and community. In: S. Ratneshwar, D. G. Mick & C. Huffman (Eds.). The Why of Consumption – Contemporary perspectives on consumer motives, goals, and desires (pp. 140-163). London: Routledge.

Avery, Jill, Sharon Betty, Morris B. Holbrook, Robert V. Kozinets, Banwari Mittal, Priya Raghubir, and Arch Woodside (2010). Consumer Behavior – Human Pursuit of Happiness in the World of Goods. Cincinnati: Open Mentis.

Bagozzi, Richard (1992). The self-regulation of attitudes, intention, and behavior. Social Psychology Quarterly, 55 (2), 178-204.

Bagozzi, Richard and Youjae Yi (1988). On the evaluation of structural equation models. Journal of the Academy of Marketing Science, 16 (Spring), 74-94.

Baker, W. H., Hutchinson, W. J., Moore, D., and Nedungadi, P. (1986). Brand Familiarity and Advertising: Effects on the Evoked set and Brand Preference. Advances in Consumer Research, 13, 637-642.

Baldwin, C., Hienerth, C., and von Hippel, E. (2006): How user innovations become commercial products: A theoretical investigation and case study. Research Policy, 35, 1291-1313.

Baron, Reuben M. and David A. Kenny (1986). The Moderator-Mediator Variable Disinction in Social Psychological Research: Conceptual, Strategic, and Statistical Considerations. Journal of Personality and Social Psychology, 51 (6), 1173-82.

Barry, T. F. and Howard, D. J. (1990). A Review and Critique of the Hierarchy of Effects in Advertising. International Journal of Advertising, 9, 121-135.

Barwise, Patrick and Meehan, Sean (2010). The One Thing You Must Get Right When Building a Brand. Harvard Business Review, 88 (12), 80-84.

Beatty, S. E. and Talpade, S. (1994). Adolescent Influence in Family Decision Making: A Replication with Extension. Journal of Consumer Research, 21, 332-341.

Belk, Russel (1988). Possessions and the Extended Self. Journal of Consumer Research, 17 (2), 127-140.

Bengtsson, Anders and Jacob Ostberg (2004). Co-Constructing Brand Equity: Consumer and Brand Managers. In: European Marketing Academy Annual Conference: European Marketing Academy.

Bernoff, J. and Li, C. (2008). Harnessing the Power of the Oh-So-Social Web. MIT Sloan Management Review, 49, 36-42.

Berthon, P., Pitt, L. F. and Campell, C. (2008). When Customers Create the Ad. California Management Review, 50, 6-30.

Bettman, J. R. and Park, C. W. (1980). Effects of Prior Knowledge and Experience and Phase of the Choice Process on Consumer Decision Processes: A Protocol Analysis. Journal of Consumer Research, 7, 234-248.

Beverland, M. B., Farrelly, F., and Quester, P. G. (2010). Authentic subcultural membership: Antecedents and consequences of authenticating acts and authoritative performances. Psychology & Marketing, 27, 698-716.

Bonsu, S. K. and Darmody, A. (2008). Co-creating Second Life. Journal of Macromarketing, 28, 355-368.

Bourdieu, Pierre (1984). Distinctions: A Social Critique of the Judgment of Taste. Cambridge, MA: Harvard University Press.

Bourdieu, Pierre (1986). The Forms of Capital. In: Handbook of Theory and Research for the Sociology of Education, J.E. Richardson, ed. New York: Greenwood.

Brown, J. J. and Reingen, P. H. (1987). Social Ties and Word-of-Mouth Referral Behavior*. Journal of Consumer Research, 14, 350-362.

Brown, J., Broderick, A. J. and Lee, N. (2007). Word of mouth communication within online communities: Conceptualizing the online social network. Journal of Interactive Marketing (John Wiley & Sons), 21, 2-20.

Brown, S., Kozinets, R., and Sherry, J. F. J. (2003). Teaching Old Brands New Tricks: Retro Branding and the Revivial of Brand Meaning. Journal of Marketing, 67, 19-33.

Browne, Michael W. and Cudeck, Robert (1993). Alternative ways of assessing model fit. In: Bollen, K. A. and Long, S. J. (eds.). Testing structural equation models. Newbury Park: Sage Publications, 136-162.

Burnham, Kenneth P. and David R. Anderson (2004). Multimodel Inference: Understanding AIC and BIC in model selection. Sociological Methods Research, 33 (2), 261-304.

Carroll, Barbara C. and Aaron C. Ahuvia (2006). Some antecedents and outcomes of brand love. Marketing Letters 17 (2), 79-89.

Castronova, E. (2005). Synthetic Worlds: The Business and Culture of Online Games, University of Chicago Press, Chicago.

Chakravarti, A., Janiszewski, C., Mick, D. G., and Hoyer, W. D. (2003). The Influence of Macro-Level Motives on Consideration Set Composition in Novel Purchase Situations. Journal of Consumer Research, 30, 244-258.

Chang, Tung-Zong and Albert R. Wildt (1994). Price, Product Information, and Purchase Intention: An Empirical Study. Journal of the Academy of Marketing Science, 22 (1), 16-27.

Chen, Yubo, Fay, Scott, and Wang, Qi (2011). The Role of Marketing in Social Media: How Online Consumer Reviews Evolve. Journal of Interactive Marketing, 25 (2), 85-94.

Chen, Yubo, Wang, Qi, and Xie, J. (2011). Online Social Interactions: A Natural Experiment on Word of Mouth Versus Observational Learning. Journal of Marketing Research (JMR), 48, 238-254.

Chesney, T., Coyne, I., Logan, B., and Madden, N. (2009). Griefing in virtual worlds: causes, casualties and coping strategies. Information Systems Journal, 19, 525-548.

Constantinides, Efthymios and Fountain, Stefan. J. (2008). Web 2.0: Conceptual foundations and marketing issues. Journal of Direct, Data and Digital Marketing Practice, 9 (3), 231-44.

Court, D. C., French, T. D., and Knudsen, T. R. (2006). The Proliferation Challenge. In: Webb, A. P. (ed.) Profiting from Proliferation. New York: McKinsey & Company.

Cova, B. and White, T. (2010). Counter-brand and alter-brand communities: the impact of Web 2.0 on tribal marketing approaches. Journal of Marketing Management, 26, 256-270.

Cova, Bernard (1997). Community and Consumption: Towards a Definition of the Linking Value of Products or Services. European Journal of Marketing, 31 (3/4), 297-316.

Cova, Bernard and Cova, Véronique (2002). Tribal marketing – The tribalisation of society and its impact on the conduct of marketing. European Journal of Marketing, 36, (5/6), 595-620.

Cova, Bernard and Pace, S. (2006). Brand community of convenience products: new forms of customer empowerment – the case "my Nutella The Community". European Jounal of Marketing, 40, 1087-1105.

Cova, Bernard, Dalli, D., and Zwick, D. (2011). Critical perspectives on consumers' role as 'producers': Broadening the debate on value co-creation in marketing processes. Marketing Theory, 11(3), 231-241.

Cova, Bernard, Kozinets, R. V. & Shankar, A. (2007). Consumer Tribes, Elsevier/Butterworth Heinemann, Amsterdam.

Day, George S. (2011). Closing the Marketing Capabilities Gap. Journal of Marketing, 75 (4), 183-95.

De Mesa, A. (2007). Virtual-World Branding: For Real? 11 November 2009. http://www.brandchannel.com/features_effect.asp?pf_id=358.

De Mesa, A. (2009). Brand Avatar: Translating virtual world branding into real world success, Palgrave Macmillan, New York.

Dennhardt, S., Kohler, T., and Füller, J. (2011). User-Generated Brands: What Brand Management Can Learn From Virtual Worlds. In European Marketing Academy 40th Conference Proceedings. Ljubljana, Slovenia.

Diamond, N., Sherry, J. F., Muniz, A. M., Mcgrath, M. A., Kozinets, R. V., and Borghini, S. (2009). American Girl and the Brand Gestalt: Closing the Loop on Sociocultural Branding Research. Journal of Marketing, 73, 118-134.

Divol, R., Edelman, D., and Sarrazin, H. (2012). Demystifying social media [Online]. McKinsey Quarterly. Available: http://www.mckinseyquarterly.com/Demystifying_social_media_2958 [Accessed 05.05.2012.

Dmd, Story, C. & Truths, M. (2007). The virtual brand footprint: the marketing opportunity in Second Life. 25 November 2012. http://popcha.com/combinedstory_whitepaper.pdf.

Dodds, W. B., Monroe, K. B., and Grewal, D. (1991). Effects of Price, Brand, and Store Information on Buyers' Product Evaluations. Journal of Marketing Research (JMR), 28, 307-319.

Douglas, Mary and Baron C. Isherwood (1996). The World of Goods: Towards an anthropology of consumption. New York: Routledge.

Edelman, D. C. (2010). Branding in the Digital Age - You're Spending Your Money In All the Wrong Places. Harvard Business Review, 88, 62-69.

Elliott, Richard (1994). Exploring the Symbolic Meaning of Brands. British Journal of Management, 5, 13-19.

Elliott, Richard and Wattanasuwan, Kritsadarat (1998). Consumption and the Symbolic Project of the Self. European Advances in Consumer Research, 3, 17-20.

12 References

Ellison, N. B., Steinfield, C., and Lampe, C. (2007). The benefits of Facebook "friends": Social capital and college students' use of online social network sites. Journal of Computer-Mediated Communication, 12, 1143-1168.

Engagementdb (2009). The world's most valuable brands. Who's most engaged? (accessed 24 November, 2009), [available at http://www.engagementdb.com/downloads/ENGAGEMENTdb_Report_2009.pdf].

Erdem, Tuelin and Swait, Joffre (1998). Brand Equity as a Signaling Phenomenon. Journal of Consumer Psychology (Lawrence Erlbaum Associates), 7 (2), 131-57.

Erdem, Tuelin and Swait, Joffre (2004). Brand Credibility, Brand Consideration, and Choice. Journal of Consumer Research, 31, 191-198.

Escalas, Jennifer Edson and Bettman, James R. (2005). Self-Construal, Reference Groups, and Brand Meaning. Journal of Consumer Research, 32 (3), 378-89.

Esser, Hartmut (2008). The two meanings of social capital. In: The Handbook of Social Capital, Dario Castiglione and Jan W. van Deth and Guglielmo Wolleb, eds. Oxford: Oxford University Press.

Farquhar, Peter H. (1990). Managing Brand Equity. Journal of Advertising Research, 30 (4), RC-7-RC-12.

Fischer, M., Völckner, F., and Sattler, H. (2010). How Important Are Brands? A Cross-Category, Cross-Country Study. Journal of Marketing Research, 47(5), 823-839.

Fornell, C. and Larcker, D. F. (1981). Evaluating structural equation models with unobservable variables and measurement error. Journal of Marketing Research, 18, 39-50.

Fournier, Susan (1998). Consumers and their brands: developing relationship theory in consumer research. Journal of Consumer Research, 24 (March), 343-73.

Franke, N. and Piller, F. (2004). Value Creation by Toolkits for User Innovation and Design. Journal of Product Innovation Management, 21 (6), 401-415.

Franke, N. and Shah, S. (2003). How Communities Support Innovative Activities: An Exploration of Assistance and Sharing Among Innovative Users of Sporting Equipment. Research Policy, 32 (1), 157-178.

Fuchs, Christoph, Emanuela Prandelli, and Martin Schreier (2010). The Psychological Effects of Empowerment Strategies on Consumers' Product Demand. Journal of Marketing, 74 (1), 65-79.

Füller, J. and Von Hippel, E. (2008). Costless Creation of Strong Brands by User Communities: Implications for Producer-Owned Brands. MIT Sloan Research Paper No. 4718-08.

Füller, J., Lüdicke, M. K., and Jawecki, G. (2007). How Brands Enchant: Insights From Observing Community Driven Brand Creation. In: Research, A. F. C. (Ed.). Annual North American Conference, Memphis, USA.

Füller, J., Schroll, R., Dennhardt, S., and Hutter, K. (2012). Social Brand Value and the Value enhancing Role of Social Media Relationships for Brands. Proceedings of the

45 Annual Hawaii International Conference of System Sciences (CD-ROM), Maui, Hawaii. Computer Society Press, 10.

Gardiner, B. (2007). No Shortcuts to Success for Virtual Entrepreneurs. 25 March 2010. http://www.wired.com/techbiz/people/news/2007/11/terdiman?currentPage=all.

Gibson, J. J. (1979). The Ecological Approach to Perception, Houghton Mifflin, London.

Gilmore, J. H. and Pine, J. B. (2007). What consumers really want – Authenticity. Boston, MA: Harvard Business School Press

Glaser, B. and Strauss, A. (1967). The discovery of grounded theory: Strategies for qualitative research, Aldine, Chicago.

Goyette, I., Ricard, L., Bergeron, J., and Marticotte, F. (2010). e-WOM Scale: Word-of-Mouth Measurement Scale for e-Services Context. Canadian Journal of Administrative Sciences (John Wiley & Sons, Inc.), 27, 5-23.

Hair, J., Black, B., Babin, B., Anderson, R., and Tatham, R. (2006). Multivariate Data Analysis, Upper Saddle River, NJ, Prentice Hall.

Hassouneh, D. and Brengman, M. (2011). Virtual worlds: a gateway for SMEs toward internationalization. Journal of Brand Management, 19, 72-90.

Hemp, P. (2006). Avatar-Based Marketing. Harvard Business Review, 84, 48-57.

Henderson, Alison and Bowley, Rachel (2010). Authentic dialogue? The role of "friendship" in a social media recruitment campaign. Journal of Communication Management, 14 (3), 237-257.

Hennig-Thurau, T., Gwinner, K. P., Walsh, G., and Gremler, D. D. (2004). Electronic Word-of-Mouth via Consumer-Opinion Platforms: What Motivates Consumers to Articulate Themselves on the Internet? Journal of Interactive Marketing, 18, 38-52.

Hinz, O., Skiera, B., Barrot, C., and Becker, J. U. forthcoming. Seeding Strategies for Viral Marketing: An Empirical Comparison. Journal of Marketing.

Hoffman, Donna L. and Fodor, Marek (2010). Can You Measure the ROI of Your Social Media Marketing? MIT Sloan Management Review, 52 (1), 41-49.

Hoffman, Donna L. and Novak, T. P. (2009). Flow Online: Lessons Learned and Future Prospects. Journal of Interactive Marketing, 23, 23-34.

Hollis, N. (2008). The Global Brand – How to create and develop lasting brand value in the world market, Palgrave Macmillan, New York.

Holt, Douglas B. (1998). Does Cultural Capital Structure American Consumption? Journal of Consumer Research, 25 (June), 1-25.

Holt, Douglas B. (2002). Why Do Brands Cause Trouble? A Dialectical Theory of Consumer Culture and Branding. Journal of Consumer Research, 29 (1), 70-90.

Holt, Douglas B. (2004). How Brands Become Icons: The Principles of Cultural Branding, HBS Press, Cambridge, MA.

12 References

Homburg, Christian, Koschate, Nicole, and Hoyer, Wayne D. (2005). Do Satisfied Customers Really Pay More? A Study of the Relationship Between Customer Satisfaction and Willingness to Pay. Journal of Marketing, 69 (2), 84-96.

Hopkins, L. (2009). Social Media: The New Business Communication Landscape, Ark Group, London.

Hoyer, Wayne D. and Brown, Steven P. (1990). Effects of Brand Awareness on Choice for a Common, Repeat-Purchase Product. Journal of Consumer Research, 17 (2), 141-48.

Hu, Li-Tze and Bentler, Peter M. (1999). Cutoff criteria for fit indexes in covariance structure analysis: conventional criteria versus new alternatives. Structural Equation Modeling: A Multidisciplinary Journal, 6 (1), 1-55.

Hutchby, I. (2001). Technologies, Texts and Affordances. Sociology, 32, 441-456.

In-Stat. (2010). Online Gaming and Social Networking Drives Virtual Goods Revenue Over $7 Billion in 2010. 15 December 2010. http://www.instat.com/press.asp?ID=2917&sku=IN1004659CM.

Jacoby, J. (1984). Perspectives on Information Overload. Journal of Consumer Research, 10, 432-435.

Jacoby, J., Szybillo, G. J., and Busato-Schach, J. (1977). Information Acquisition Behavior in Brand Choice Situations. Journal of Consumer Research, 3, 209-216.

Jang, H., Olfman, L., Ko, I., Koh, J., and Kim, K. (2008). The Influence of On-Line Brand Community Characteristics on Community Commitment and Brand Loyalty. International Journal of Electronic Commerce, 12, 57-80.

Jones, M. R. and Karsten, H. (2008). Giddens's structuration theory and information systems research. MIS Quarterly, 32, 127-157.

Kamakura, Wagner A. and Russell, Gary J. (1993). Measuring brand value with scanner data. International Journal of Research in Marketing, 10 (1), 9-22.

Kane, G. C., Fichman, R. G., Gallaugher, J., and Glaser, J. (2009). Community Relations 2.0. Harvard Business Review, 87, 45-50.

Kapferer, Jean-Noel (2008). The New Strategic Brand Management (4th ed.). London: Kogan Page.

Kaplan, A. M. and Haenlein, M. (2010). Users of the world, unite! The challenges and opportunities of Social Media. Business Horizons, 53, 59-68.

Kates, S. M. (2004). The Dynamics of Brand Legitimacy: An Interpretive Study in the Gay Men's Community. Journal of Consumer Research, 31 (2), 455-464.

Katz, E. and Lazarsfeld, P. (1955). Personal Influence: The Part Played by People in the Flow of Mass Communications, Glencoe, IL Free Press.

Keller, Kevin Lane (1993). Conceptualizing, measuring, managing customer-based brand equity. Journal of Marketing, 57, 1-22.

Keller, Kevin Lane (2008). Strategic brand management: building, measuring, and managing brand equity (3 ed.). Upper Saddle River, NJ: Pearson Education.

Keller, Kevin Lane (2009). Building strong brands in a modern marketing communications environment. Journal of Marketing Communications, 15 (2), 139-155.

Keller, Kevin Lane and Richey, K. (2006). The importance of corporate brand personality traits to a successful 21st century business. Journal of Brand Management, 14, 74-81.

Kim, D. J., Kwok-Bun, Y., Hall, S. P., and Gates, T. (2009). Global Diffusion of the Internet XV: Web 2.0 Technologies, Principles, and Applications: A Conceptual Framework from Technology Push and Demand Pull Perspective. Communications of AIS, 2009, 657-672.

Kim, J. W., Choi, J., Qualls, W., and Han, K. (2008). It takes a marketplace community to raise brand commitment: the role of online communities. Journal of Marketing Management, 24, 409-431.

Klaassen, A. (2006). Major turnoff: McKinsey slams TV's selling power. (cover story). Advertising Age, 77, 1-33.

Kline, Rex B. (1998). Principles and Practice of Structural Equation Modeling, New York, Guilford Press.

Kohler, T., Fueller, J., Matzler, K. & Stieger, D. (2011). Co-Creation in Virtual Worlds: The Design of the User Experience. MIS Quarterly, 35, 773-788.

Kotler, P. (1997). Marketing Management: analysis, planning, implementation, and control, Prentice -Hall, New Jersey.

Kotler, P. and Bliemel, F. (2001). Marketing-Managementment, Stuttgart, Schäffer-Poeschel Verlag.

Kozinets, Robert V. (2002). Can Consumers Escape the Market? Emancipatory Illuminations from Burning Man. Journal of Consumer Research, 29 (1), 20-38.

Kozinets, Robert V., De Valck, K., Wojnicki, A. C., and Wilner, S. J. S. (2010). Networked Narratives: Understanding Word-of-Mouth Marketing in Online Communities. Journal of Marketing, 74 (2), 71-89.

Kozinets, Robert V., Hemetsberger, Andrea, and Schau, Hope J. (2008). The Wisdom of Consumer Crowds: Collective Innovation in the Age of Networked Marketing. Journal of Macromarketing, 28 (4), 339-354.

La Ferla, R. (2009). No Budget, No Boundaries: It's the Real You. 29 October 2009. http://www.nytimes.com/2009/10/22/fashion/22Avatar.html?_r=1.

Lavidge, R. J. and Steiner, G. A. (1961). A Model for Predictive Measurements of Advertising Effectiveness. Journal of Marketing, 25, 59-62.

Lee, J. and McGowan, K. M. (1998). Direct Marketing Solicitatinos: Do they Generate Sales or Consumer Annoyance? Journal of Marketing Management (10711988), 8, 63-71.

Lin, Nan (2001). Building a Network Theory of Social Capital. In: Lin, Nan, Cook, Karen, and Burt, Ronald S. (Eds.). Social Capital – Theory and Research. Hawthorne, NY: Aldine de Gruyter.

Liu, Y. (2006). Word of Mouth for Movies: Its Dynamics and Impact on Box Office Revenue. Journal of Marketing, 70, 74-89.

Luedicke, Marius K., Thompson, Craig J. and Giesler, Markus (2010). Consumer Identity Work as Moral Protagonism: How Myth and Ideology Animate a Brand-Mediated Moral Conflict. Journal of Consumer Research, 36 (6), 1016-32.

Lüthje, C., Herstatt, C., and von Hippel, E. (2005). User-innovators and "local" information: The case of mountain biking. Research Policy, 34 (6), 951-965.

Mackenzie, S. B., Podsakoff, P. M., and Paine, J. B. (1999). Do Citizenship Behaviors Matter More for Managers than for Salespeople? Journal of the Academy of Marketing Science, 27, 396-410.

Macmillan, D. (2007). Virtual World Rich List. 25 March 2010. http://images.businessweek.com/ss/07/04/0416_richlist/index_01.htm.

Mathwick, Charla, Wiertz, Caroline and De Ruyter, Ko (2008). Social Capital Production in a Virtual P3 Community. Journal of Consumer Research, 34 (6), 832-49.

Maxwell, J. (2008). Designing a qualitative study. In: Bickman, L. and Rog, D. J. (Eds.) The SAGE Handbook of Applied Social Research Methods. Thousand Oaks: Sage Publications.

McAlexander, James H., Kim, Stephen K. and Roberts, Scott D. (2003). Loyalty: The Influence of Satisfaction and Brand Community Integration. Journal of Marketing Theory & Practice, 11 (4), 1-11.

McAlexander, James H., Schouten, John, and Koenig, Harold (2002). Building Brand Community. Journal of Marketing, 66 (1), 38-54.

McCoy, S., Everard, A., Polak, P., and Galleta, D. F. (2007). The Effects of Online Advertising. Communications of the ACM, 50, 84-88.

McCracken, G. (1989). Who Is the Celebrity Endorser? Cultural Foundations of the Endorsement Process. Journal of Consumer Research, 16 (3), 310-321.

Mennecke, B., Mcneill, D., Ganis, M., Roche, E. M., Bray, D. A., Konsynski, B., Townsend, A. M., and Lester, J. (2009). Second Life and Other Virtual Worlds: A Roadmap for Research (Follow-Up Article to the 2007 International Conference on Information Systems Panel). Communications of the Association for Information Systems, Vol. 18, No. 28, 2008.

Merz, Michael A., Yi, He, and Vargo, Stephen L. (2009). The Evolving Brand Logic: A Service-Dominant Logic Perspective. Journal of the Academy of Marketing Science, 37 (3), 328-344.

Mooney, Kelly and Rollins, Nita (2008). The Open Brand: When Push Comes to Pull in an Web-Made World. Berkeley: New Riders.

Mooradian, T., Matzler, K., and Ring, L. J. (2012). Strategic Marketing, Upper Saddle River, NJ, Prentice Hall.

Morgan, R. M. and Hunt, S. D. (1994). The Commitment-Trust Theory of Relationship Marketing. Journal of Marketing, 58, 20-38.

Mueller, J., Hutter, K., Fueller, J., and Matzler, K. (2011). Virtual worlds as knowledge management platform – a practice-perspective. Information Systems Journal, 21, 479-501.

Mühlbacher, H. and Hemetsberger, A. (2008). Cosa diamine é un brand? Un tentativo di integrazione e le sueconseguenze per la ricerca e il management. Micro & Macro Marketing, 271-292.

Muniz, A. M. and O'Guinn, T. (2001). Brand Community. Journal of Consumer Research, 27 (4), 412-432.

Muniz, A. M. and Schau, H. J. (2005). Religiosity in the Abondened Apple Newton Brand Community. Journal of Consumer Research, 31, 737-747.

Muniz, A. M. and Schau, H. J. (2007). Vigilante Marketing and Consumer-Created Communications. Journal of Advertising, 36, 35-50.

Naylor, R. W., Lamberton, C. P., and West, P. M. (2012). Beyond the "Likeâ" Button: The Impact of Mere Virtual Presence on Brand Evaluations and Purchase Intentions in Social Media Settings. Journal of Marketing, 76, 105-120.

Norman, D. A. (2004). Affordance, Convention and Design. 15 July 2012. http://www.jnd.org/dn.mss/affordance_conventi.html.

OECD (2007). Participative Web: User-created content. Working Party on the Information Economy. Organisation for Economic Co-operation and Development.

Ohanian, R. (1990). Construction and Validation of a Scale to Measure Celebrity Endorsers' Perceived Expertise, Trustworthiness, and Attractiveness. Journal of Advertising, 19, 39-52.

Olshavsky, R. W. and Granbois, D. H. (1979). Consumer Decision Making – Fact or Fiction? Journal of Consumer Research, 6, 93-100.

Ondrejka, C. (2004). Escaping the Gilded Cage: User Created Content and Building the Metaverse. Working Paper, New York Law School, retrieved October 2006, from http://ssrn.com/abstract=538362.

Pappu, Ravi, Quester, Pascale G. and. Cooksey, Ray W. (2005). Consumer-based brand equity: improving the measurement. Journal of Product & Brand Management, 14 (3), 143-54.

Park, Chan Su and Srinivasan, V. (1994). A survey-based method for measuring and understanding brand equity and its extendibility. Journal of Marketing Research, 31 (2), 271-88.

Peterson, N. Andrew, Speer, Paul W., and McMillan, David W. (2008). Validation of A brief sense of community scale: Confirmation of the principal theory of sense of community. Journal of Community Psychology, 36 (1), 61-73.

Petty, R. E., Cacioppo, J. T., and Schumann, D. (1983). Central and Peripheral Routes to Advertising Effectiveness: The Moderating Role of Involvement. Journal of Consumer Research, 10, 135-146.

Pitt, L. F., Watson, R. T., Berthon, P., Wynn, D., and Zinkhan, G. M. (2006). The Penguin's Window: Corporate Brand From an Open-Source Perspective. Journal of the Academy of Marketing Science, 34 (2), 115-127.

Podsakoff, P. M., Mackenzie, S. B., Lee, J.-Y., and Podsakoff, N. P. (2003). Common Method Biases in Behavioral Research: A Critical Review of the Literature and Recommended Remedies. Journal of Applied Psychology, 88, 879-903.

Preacher, Kristopher J. and Hayes, Andrew F. (2004). SPSS and SAS procedures for estimating indirect effects in simple mediation models. Behavior Research Methods, Instruments, & Computers, 36 (4), 717-31.

Preacher, Kristopher J. and Hayes, Andrew F. (2008). Asymptotic and resampling strategies for assessing and comparing indirect effects in multiple mediator models. Behavior Research Methods, 40 (3), 879-91.

Qualman, Eric (2011). Socialnomics – how social media transforms the way we live and do business. New Jersey: Wiley & Sons.

Rangaswamy, Arvind, Burke, Raymond R. and Oliva, Terence A. (1993). Brand equity and the extendibility of brand names. International Journal of Research in Marketing, 10 (3), 61-75.

Rao, Akshay R. and Bergen, Mark E. (1992). Price Premium Variations as a Consequence of Buyers' Lack of Information. Journal of Consumer Research, 19 (3), 412-23.

Ray, M. (1973). Marketing Communications and the Hierarchy-of-Effects. In: Clarke, P. (Ed.). New Models for Mass Communications. Beverly Hills, CA: Sage Publications.

Read, S., Dew, N., Sarasvathy, S. D., Song, M., and Wiltbank, R. (2009). Marketing Under Uncertainty: The Logic of an Effectual Approach. Journal of Marketing 73, 1-18.

Richins, M. L. (1983). An Analysis of Consumer Interaction Styles in the Marketplace. Journal of Consumer Research, 10, 73-82.

Richins, Marsha (1994). Valuing Things: The Public and Private Meanings of Possessions. Journal of Consumer Research, 21 (3), 504-21.

Riesenbeck, H. and Perrey, J. (2007). Power Brands – Measuring, Making, Managing Brand Succes, Wiley, Weinheim.

Roselius, R. (1971). Consumer Rankings of Risk Reduction Methods. Journal of Marketing, 35, 56-61.

Ruyter, Ko de, Wetzels, Martin, and Bloemer, Josee (1998). On the relationship between perceived service quality, service loyalty and switching costs. International Journal of Service Industry Management, 9 (5), 436.

Sawhney, M., Verona, G., and Prandelli, E. (2005). Collaborating to create: The Internet as a platform for customer engagement in product innovation. Journal of Interactive Marketing, 19.

Scammon, D. L. (1977). "Information Load" and Consumers. Journal of Consumer Research, 4, 148-155.

Schau, Hope Jensen, Muniz, Albert M., and Arnould, Eric J. (2009). How Brand Community Practices Create Value. Journal of Marketing, 73 (5), 30-51.

Schroll, R., Hemetsberger, A., and Füller, J. (2010). „Fine feathers make fine birds" – Community Brands and Branded Communities. Advances in Consumer Research, 38.

Shah, S. K. and Smith, S. W. (2010). Intellectual Property, Prior Knowledge & the Survival of New Firms. Paper presented on the Entrepreneurship Research Conference, University of Maryland, USA.

Shah, S. K. and Tripsas, M. (2007). The Accidental Entrepreneur: The Emergent and Collective Process of User Entrepreneurship. Strategic Entrepreneurship Journal, 1, 123-140.

Shocker, A. D. and Weitz, B. (1988). A perspective on brand equity principles and issues. Report No 88-104 (Cambridge, MA: Marketing Science Institute).

Smith, R. E., Chen, J., and Yang, X. (2008). The Impact of Advertising Creativity on the Hierarchy of Effects. Journal of Advertising, 37, 47-61.

Smith, T. (2009). The social media revolution. International Journal of Market Research, 51, 559-561.

Solomon, M. R. (1983). The Role of Products as Social Stimuli: A Symbolic Interactionism Perspective. Journal of Consumer Research, 10 (3), 319-29.

Solomon, M. R. (2011). Consumer Behavior – Buying, Having and Being, Upper Saddle River, NJ, Pearson.

Srivastava, R. K. and Shocker, A. D. (1991). Brand equity: A perspective on its meaning and measurement. Cambridge.

Stake, R. E. (1995). The Art of Case Study Research, Sage Publications.

Strauss, A. and Corbin, J. (1990). Basics of Qualitative Research: Techniques and Procedures for Developing Grounded Theory, Sage Publications, Newbury Park, Calif.

Tamborini, R., Bowman, N. D., Eden, A., Grizzard, M., and Organ, A. (2010). Defining Media Enjoyment as the Satisfaction of Intrinsic Needs. Journal of Communication, 60, 758-777.

Taylor, Steven A. and Baker, Thomas L. (1994). An assessment of the relationship between service quality and customer satisfaction. Journal of Retailing, 70 (2), 163-78.

The Brand Report Card (2000). Article. Directed by Keller, K. L.: Harvard Business School Publication Corp.

Thompson, C. J., Rindfleisch, A., and Arsel, Z. (2006). Emotional Branding and the Strategic Value of the Doppelgänger Brand Image. Journal of Marketing 70(1), 50-64.

Tian, K. T., Bearden, W. O., and Hunter, G. L. (2001). Consumers' Need for Uniqueness: Scale Development and Validation. Journal of Consumer Research, 28, 50-66.

Toennis, Ferdinand (1988). Gemeinschaft und Gesellschaft. Darmstadt: Wiss. Buchges.

Vakratsas, D. and Ambler, T. (1999). How Advertising Works: What Do We Really Know? Journal of Marketing, 63, 26-43.

Vargo, Stephen L. and Lusch, Robert F. (2004). Evolving to a New Dominant Logic for Marketing. Journal of Marketing, 68 (1), 1-17.

Vargo, Stephen L. and Lusch, Robert F. (Article directed by them) (2008). Service-dominant logic: continuing the evolution. Springer Science & Business Media B.V.

Vogt, Ludgera (2000). Identität und Kapital – Über den Zusammenhang von Identitätsoptionen und sozialer Ungleichheit. In: Hettlage, Robert and Vogt, Ludgera (Eds.). Identitäten in der Modernen Welt. Wiesbaden: Westdeutscher Verlag, 77-100.

Von Hippel, E. (1988). The sources of innovation. New York: Oxford University Press.

Von Hippel, E. (2005). Democratizing Innovation, MIT Press, Cambridge, MA.

Von Hippel, E., Schroll, R., and Füller, J. (2011). Brands as User Generated Content: Evidence and Implications. SSRN eLibrary.

Wells, J. D., Valacich, J. S., and Hess, T. J. (2011). What Signal are you Sending? How Website Quality Influences Perceptions od Product Quality and Purchase Intentions. MIS Quarterly, 35, 373-A18.

Wipperfürth, A. (2005). Brand Hijack: Marketing Without Marketing, Portfolio, New York, NY.

Wood, A. M., Linley, P. A., Maltby, J., Baliousis, M., and Joseph, S. (2008). The Authentic Personality: A Theoretical and Empirical Conceptualization and the Development of the Authenticity Scale. Journal of Counseling Psychology, 55, 385-399.

Yin, R. K. (2009). Case Study Research: Design and Methods, Sage Publications.

Yoo, B., Donthu, N., and Lee, S. (2000). An Examination of Selected Marketing Mix Elements and Brand Equity. Journal of the Academy of Marketing Science, 28, 195-211.

Zaichkowsky, J. L. (1985). Measuring the Involvement Construct. Journal of Consumer Research, 12, 341-352.

Zeithaml, Valerie A., Leonard L. Berry, and A. Parasuraman (1988). Communication and Control Process in the Delivery of Service Quality. Journal of Marketing, 52 (2), 35-48.

Zhu, Feng and Zhang, Xiaoquan (2010). Impact of Online Consumer Reviews on Sales: The Moderating Role of Product and Consumer Characteristics. Journal of Marketing, 74 (2), 133-48.

Article Overview

Nr.	References
1	Dennhardt, S; Kohler, T.; Füller, J. (*under review*). User-generated Brands Emerging from Social Media: What Corporate Brands can Learn from Brand Management in Virtual Worlds, Information Systems Journal.
2	Dennhardt, S. (2012). Perception of user-generated brands: a new power in the minds of consumers?, Proceedings of the 19th International Products development Management Conference (IPDMC), Manchester, June 17-19.
3	Füller, J.; Dennhardt, S.; Schroll, R; Hutter, K. (*under review*). The Value-Enhancing Role of Social Networks Around Brands: The Concept of Social Brand Value, Journal of Marketing.
4	Hautz, J.; Dennhardt, S.; Füller, J.; Hutter, K. (*under review*). The impact of social media on brand awareness and purchase intention: the case of MINI on Facebook, 41st European Marketing Academy Conference (EMAC).

Druck: KN Digital Printforce GmbH · Schockenriedstraße 37 · 70565 Stuttgart